The Shoshoni Cook

Vegetarian Recipes
from the
Shoshoni Yoga Retreat

by Anne Saks
&
Faith Stone

Book Publishing Company
Summertown, Tennessee

Published in the United States by
The Book Publishing Company, P.O. Box 99
Summertown, TN 38483

Front cover photo: *Masala Dosa*, pg. 124, *Coconut Mint Chutney*, pg. 89

Cover photos by Ron Coppock
Foodstyling by Kathryn Arnold
Cover and interior design by Barbara McNew
Editing by Sue Frederick

Many thanks to Charlotte Vandenburg, Lisa Stone, Ken Fowler, Tait
Christensen, and Charlotte Brownlee for their creative contributions;
to Sue Frederick, Andrea Ahrens, and Chris Davies for their tireless
editing; and to the entire Shoshoni staff for their loving support
throughout the writing of this book.

Library of Congress Cataloging-in-Publication Data
Saks, Anne, 1957-
    The Shoshoni cookbook : vegetarian recipes from the Shoshoni Yoga
Retreat / by Anne Saks & Faith Stone.
        p. cm.
    Includes index.
    ISBN 0-913990-49-3
    1. Vegetarian cookery. 2. Cookery, Yoga. 3. Shoshoni Yoga Retreat.
I. Stone, Faith, 1954-   . II. Shoshoni Yoga Retreat. III. Title
TX837.S237 1993
641.5'636--dc20   93-8782
                                                   CIP

ISBN 0-913990-49-3
0 9 8 7 6 5 4 3

Calculations for the nutritional analyses in this book are based on the average number of servings
listed with the recipes and the average amount of an ingredient if a range is listed. Calculations
are rounded up to the nearest gram. If two options for an ingredient are listed, the first one is used.
Not included are optional ingredients, serving suggestions, or fat used for frying, unless the
amount is specified in the recipe.

We dedicate this book with love and gratitude
to our teacher, Shambhavananda Yogi.

Meet Anne and Faith

In 1980, Anne Saks first came to study yoga with Shambhavananda Yogi. She immediately became an apprentice at Rudi's Restaurant—studying under the guidance of master chef Faith Stone. For ten years at Rudi's, Anne learned the fine nuances of gourmet natural foods cooking, extending that training to run the Ashram kitchen as well. As manager of the Shoshoni Yogi Retreat kitchen, she planned all the meals and prepared fine food for the many Shoshoni visitors and staff. "It has been a spiritual training ground to run the kitchen at Shoshoni," she says. "Cooking is creative and it serves other people. It has been the arena for learning things that people spend lifetimes and fortunes seeking." Today she still cooks at Shoshoni and for her husband and daughter, Dominique.

In 1975, Faith Stone and Swami Shambhavananda opened Rudi's Restaurant in Boulder to serve tasty, fresh, wholesome foods prepared with grace and love. Today, Rudi's is a Boulder landmark, and Faith's many delicious creations attract people from all over the region. She cooks for visitors and staff at Shoshoni Yoga Retreat, teaches cooking classes in the Boulder/Denver area and is also a member of the American Culinary Federation. Considered a pioneer in the Boulder gourmet vegetarian scene, she is also a very advanced student of yoga and the mother of a beautiful little girl, Tara.

Table of Contents

INTRODUCTION

About Shoshoni

Shoshoni Yoga Retreat, named after nearby Shoshoni Mountain, rests on 210 acres of colorful Colorado high country--surrounded by lush national forest. Our land has a friendly, joyful quality. Bright prayer flags and large Buddhas painted on rock walls adorn the valley much as one would see in India or Tibet. Log cabins nestled in the forest provide rustic charm with all the comforts of home for our guests.

A day at Shoshoni begins with morning meditation and chanting followed by a hearty, healthful breakfast. Our cuisine is low-fat, vegetarian, and very tasty. After a day of yoga, meditation, hiking, and massage, guests often relax in the hot tub or doze on the deck overlooking Little Bear Mountain. Dinners are often shared outside on the spacious deck overlooking nearby snow-capped peaks.

It is remarkable to watch the change in visitors as the Shoshoni environment strips away years of tightness and tension from their bodies and minds. Many guests attribute the change to the pristine mountain air, the pure spring water, and the incredible food. The resident yogis know it is the meditative energy (or Shakti) which heals, cleanses, and restores people. And this energy is put into every dish prepared in the Shoshoni kitchen.

About Our Teacher

Eldorado Mountain Yoga Ashram and Shoshoni Yoga Retreat were founded by Shambhavananda Yogi. He is a radiant, big-hearted teacher who is a master of Kundalini Yoga. He teaches a method for meditation and growth called Shambhava Yoga. His vision for Eldorado and Shoshoni is to create an environment conducive to inner growth which nurtures practitioners toward the realization of their true Self or Buddha nature. Facilities include residential areas for full-time yogis, non-resident classes, and retreat or visitor facilities.

Shambhavananda is rightly described by the name: Shambhav-ananda, which means the bliss of the natural state. His method of training students of yoga is unencumbered by dogma. He relates to the latent spiritual energy within aspirants, not to their limited view of themselves. Sri Nityananda, our root Guru, taught, "The heart is the hub of all sacred places. Go there and roam in it." It is this holy place within which Shambhavananda encourages seekers to explore.

The Shoshoni Kitchen

The Shoshoni kitchen is a fascinating place. It was once a kitchen for a summer camp that served hundreds of children. Central to the kitchen is a new shiny stove with two large ovens surrounded by giant, stainless steel pots, pans, cast iron skillets, and hanging spoons and ladles. Five-gallon buckets overflow with various beans, grains, and colorful fresh vegetables. Quart jars brim with aromatic spices and herbs. Come on in and spend some time with our chefs.

Before daybreak, the breakfast cook enters the kitchen, lights the devotional candle, and puts on a chanting tape. Her quiet voice follows the chant as she hoists a large, stainless steel pot onto the flame. In go the oats, the water, and the masala, and Indian Cereal is started. Fresh muffins, toast, and fruit are prepared as she dances like a Shiva before dawn.

The Shoshoni staff works together to clean up after each meal. Guests love to join in the clean-up activities when a joyful family feeling makes work fun. After a brief morning meeting, the lunch cooks review the menu and plan for the day. Last minute changes are almost always made to include the unexpected, such as the arrival of fresh picked greens from the Eldorado Ashram. Today's lunch will be Spanakopita, Fragrant Rice Salad, and Savory Lentils. The chanting continues, creating a light atmosphere where the cooks focus on their work, repeating mantras as lunch is prepared.

Yogiji often enters the kitchen close to mealtime and tastes each dish. He takes a spoonful sample and a deep, inwardly focused breath. He immediately knows what it needs and, like a magician, transforms the food into nectar. The food is offered to Sri Nityananda, our root Guru, with a blessing chant, then served to a hungry group who just finished a Hatha Yoga class or chanting.

When we have a full house at Shoshoni, the kitchen is a hub of activity. Mountains of fresh vegetables are chopped with one-pointed perfection. We all wonder how we got it done. Somehow the Shakti, or meditative energy, took over and the results are delicious Shoshoni meals.

Shoshoni's two master cooks, Faith Stone and Anne Saks, who created these delicious recipes, believe the most important ingredient in any dish is the heartfelt love put into it by the chefs.

Cooking with Shakti

People have been requesting our recipes for years. What makes the food so good? What did you put in this? How can vegetarian food taste so good? The cooks always look at each other and smile. They know that what is in the food can't be bought in the store or duplicated by the finest chefs. The magic ingredient we put into every dish is Shakti or Divine Energy. Food is treated as God because it contains the essence of life, a conscious energy that nourishes that same energy in you. The cook who seeks God in himself or herself while preparing food, cooks from a special place and adds Shakti to the food.

Simple Methods To Add Shakti To Your Food

Blessing the Food

Set aside a high, clean place in your kitchen to set up a small altar. Before serving your meal, offer it to God with a prayer or blessing chant. At Shoshoni we prepare a plate of food for the lineage teachers. We offer it up with a chant, then each item is stirred back into the original food. It is like adding a secret spice that turns the food into ambrosia.

Preparing to Cook

A very important element of cooking is the state you are in while preparing food. Anger, depression, or negativity can go into the food and give people a stomach ache. No matter how you feel, pause a moment before you start and take a deep breath. Let go of thoughts just as you do in meditation, let go of negative emotions by breathing into your heart and allowing heavy tensions to drop down the arms and out of the hands. Shake off the hands and repeat this exercise a few times while asking to release all deep negative tensions. Now, feel an openness in your heart and let that expand. Deep from within the heart a feeling of love wells up. Let that light energy flow down the arms and into the hands which are your main tools for cooking. Feeling new all through, begin to cook with a clear mind and open heart.

Mantra and Chanting in the Kitchen

Om Namah Shivayah, Om Namah Shivayah, Om Namah Shivayah, Om Namah Shivayah, Om Namah Shivayah, Om Namah Shivayah! Mantra repetition is the heartbeat of the kitchen. Mantra is sacred sound, infused with Shakti (divine energy), and repeated silently or out loud to evoke that divine energy. Mantras permeate the cooks, permeate the food, and permeate you when you eat the food. If you have been given a mantra by your teacher, use that; if not, repeat "Om Namah Shivaya," which translates as "I bow with respect to my Inner Self," while preparing food.

RECIPE FOR A YOGI

1 pound of insatiable desire to unite with God

365 days (per year) of practice

Handfuls of private retreats

Unlimited surrender

2 dashes of insanity

A sense of humor, to taste

1. Combine all. Marinate in Shakti.

2. Using one very good teacher to stir, bring to a boil, and simmer for lifetimes.

3. Serve with love and devotion.

About The Shoshoni Cookbook

All the recipes in this book have been tested at Shoshoni and received rave reviews from our guests. We selected them because they're tasty, healthful, and nourishing.

While you're trying these new dishes, please remember one important point. Whenever you're cooking, begin with the intention that what you're creating will be wonderful, and don't doubt it. Create food as an act of love, and think positively. This attitude is really more important than the tangible ingredients you use.

A lot of people feel paralyzed in the kitchen unless they have fancy ingredients such as walnut oil, balsamic vinegar, or sun-dried tomatoes. We love all of those things, however, our attitude while cooking is more important to us than the actual ingredients. Don't worry if you don't have all the ingredients called for in a recipe. Experiment. Allow yourself to be creative. Go beyond yourself and the limits of your mind: love the food and have fun. Think of these recipes as a basic outline to a wholesome dish, and add your own creative touches. Each recipe in this book may still need a pinch of salt or a dash of spice. Recipes are simply maps that give directions to a place that has been experienced before, so please feel free to create your own visions. It's best to use up what you have on hand and not to waste food.

Our teacher, Swami Shambhavananda, often talks about a yogi's ability to turn poison into food. However, many people turn food into poison with negative emotions such as anger and fear. From a yogic point of view, you can eat anything and purify it inside yourself. Most of us aren't capable of that. For us, a healthful diet provides the energy to develop other parts of our lives—such as spiritual work. At Shoshoni we believe that food can balance us and make us stronger so that we can better serve other people.

Why Vegan? Why Low-Fat?

You may notice that our recipes don't contain eggs, meat, or dairy products. Our guests don't notice anything missing from our food; in fact, they rave about its nourishing qualities.

However, we've chosen to eliminate these ingredients because it's widely acknowledged that these are the primary sources of fat and cholesterol in our diet. At Shoshoni, we want to serve only the most healthful, nourishing food—both spiritually and physically. By eliminating these ingredients, we reduce the fat by fifty percent or more in most of our recipes.

Don't be confused about our reason for reducing the fat. We aren't trying to encourage weight loss (although that happens effortlessly on this food). The latest scientific research shows that high-fat and meat-based diets are directly linked to our nation's high rates of cancer and heart disease.

We're sure you'll feel spiritually and physically better by preparing delicious, nutritious recipes such as those we've collected here. Not only are they low-fat and plant-based, but tasty too. You'll feel nourished inside and out. Enjoy!

To contact Shoshoni Yoga Retreat, write to:

P.O. Box 410

Rollinsville, CO 80474

or phone: (303) 642-0116

GLOSSARY

Agar: A clear, flavorless, freeze-dried sea vegetable used like gelatin. The recipes in this book call for agar flakes, but it is also available in bars.

Anasazi Bean: A red and white speckled bean similar to a pinto bean. Originally cultivated by Native Americans.

Arrowroot: A natural thickening agent derived from the tuber of the arrowroot plant. May be substituted for cornstarch in sauces and puddings. Should be dissolved in cold water first to prevent lumps.

Asafetida: This aromatic resin from the root of the giant fennel plant has a distinctive pungent flavor. Use minute quantities to add unique flavor to curries and dals. Powdered asafetida, also called *hing*, can be found in Indian and Asian markets.

Atta (Chapati flour): A low-gluten whole wheat flour used for Indian flatbreads. Atta is highly nutritious, as it contains the entire wheat kernel. Available in Indian and Asian groceries.

Balsamic Vinegar: A sweet, full-bodied red wine vinegar.

Basmati Rice: A light-textured, long grain, aromatic rice from North India and Pakistan with a wonderful fragrance and flavor. Basmati is typically white, but a brown variety is now available. Look for basmati rice at natural food stores, well-stocked groceries, or Asian and Indian markets.

Brown Mustard Seeds: Also known as *rai*, this is a commonly used seed spice in Indian cuisine. Fry these seeds in hot oil to release their nutty, pungent flavor before adding to curries.

Brown Rice Syrup: A thick syrup made from brown rice. Its mildly sweet taste is perfect in baked goods, desserts, and sweets as an alternative to processed sugar or honey.

Bulgur Wheat: A grain product made by parboiling and drying whole wheat kernels and crushing them into various sizes. It has a chewy texture, pleasant nutty taste, and is rich in protein, calcium, phosphorus, and iron.

Canola Oil

Canola Oil: Extracted from rapeseed, canola oil has the lowest saturated fat content of all commonly used cooking oils. We recommend it as an all-purpose vegetable oil.

Cardamom

Cardamom: The aromatic seeds from a plant grown in the tropical regions of India. Their pleasant flavor complements rice dishes, cereals, and sweets. They are also chewed as a breath freshener and digestive aid after a meal. Cardamom is available in the pod, as seeds, or as a powder.

Carob

Carob: A natural, healthful substitute for chocolate in desserts and sweets. Produced by roasting and grinding locust tree pod, it is available in powder, chips, and syrups. Carob is rich in protein and iron.

Chapati

Chapati: An unleavened flat bread. A traditional food in India, chapatis are used in place of a fork by folding the bread and scooping food.

Chick-Peas

Chick-Peas: Also known as garbanzo beans, these large, light brown peas are used extensively in many cuisines around the world.

Chinese Five-Spice Powder

Chinese Five-Spice Powder: A combination of ground cinnamon, cloves, fennel, star anise, and Szechuan peppers.

Cilantro

Cilantro: The pungent leaf of the coriander plant. Used fresh in Indian, Mexican, and Asian dishes.

Couscous

Couscous: A refined grain product made by extracting the heart of the wheat kernel (semolina). Typically used with Middle Eastern and North African dishes, couscous cooks very quickly, making it a convenient grain.

Cumin Seed

Cumin Seed: Yellowish-brown oval seeds similar in appearance to caraway. The flavor and aroma of cumin, like most seed spices, intensifies after it has been dry-roasted or fried in hot oil. Ground cumin can be used as a convenient substitute. Cumin is used extensively in Indian, Mexican, and Middle Eastern cuisine.

Dal

Dal: The name for any type of dried bean, lentil, or pea in India. Also the name for thick, gravy-like or thin, soup-like dishes prepared from these beans.

Daikon Radish

Daikon Radish: Large, white radish eaten raw, cooked, or pickled.

Egg Replacer: Made from potato starch and tapioca to replace eggs in baked goods. Fat- and cholesterol-free egg replacer can be found in health food stores.

Egg Replacer

Feta: A crumbly, strong-tasting, white cheese usually made from sheep's milk and ripened in brine.

Feta

Filo: A paper-thin pastry popular throughout the Middle East and Greece. These delicate pastry sheets must be handled with care to prevent drying. Look for filo pastry in well-stocked supermarkets, delicatessens, and health food stores.

Filo

Garam Masala: A blend of dry-roasted and ground spices used in Indian cuisine. The spices used for garam masala warm the body (garam means warm). The components vary according to the region, but usually consist of dried chilies, black pepper, cardamom, coriander, cinnamon, cloves, and cumin. Found in Indian markets and most health food stores.

Garam Masala

Jicama: A crunchy, mildly sweet Mexican root vegetable shaped like a giant beet with tan skin and white flesh. May be peeled and eaten raw or cooked.

Jicama

Kasha: Whole, roasted buckwheat groats popular in Russian and Jewish cooking. All forms of buckwheat are rich in iron, protein, and B vitamins.

Kasha

Kombu: A thick, broad-leaved sea vegetable used to flavor soups and stews. Kombu may also be added to beans to reduce cooking time and improve digestibility.

Kombu

Masa Harina: Finely ground corn flour used for making tortillas and tamales. Found in the Mexican food section of supermarkets.

Masa Harina

Masala: Any combination of herbs, spices, or seasonings used in Indian cuisine.

Masala

Mirin: Sweet Japanese cooking wine made from rice, similar to sherry. Especially good in marinades, sauces, and dressings.

Mirin

Miso

Miso: Salted and fermented paste made from soy or other beans and grains. Excellent as a base in soups and sauces or as a flavor enhancer in dips and spreads. Darker colored misos tend to be saltier and have a richer flavor than lighter misos, which have a sweeter "cheesy" flavor.

Nutritional Yeast

Nutritional Yeast: A natural flavor enhancer and nutritional supplement, rich in B vitamins, essential amino acids, and chromium.

Pine Nut

Pine Nut: Also known as pignolia, these small, cream colored kernels are extracted from the stone pine tree grown in the Mediterranean.

Pita Bread

Pita Bread: A lightly leavened, round, Middle Eastern bread with a soft crust and hollow center. Pita bread is made without oil and makes an excellent bread for sandwiches and dips.

Polenta

Polenta: A coarse yellow cornmeal used for making a baked cornmeal mush.

Pozole

Pozole: Large, dried, white corn kernels (hominy) used in making a traditional Mexican stew. Dried pozole takes 3 to 4 hours to cook. If you're unable to find pozole in the Mexican food section of your supermarket, canned hominy may be substituted.

Quinoa

Quinoa: A small, disk-shaped grain that contains up to 50% more protein than common grains. Originally grown and eaten in the Andes mountains of South America, quinoa is delicious as a side dish, salad, or added to soups and stews. Rinse well before cooking.

Rice Milk

Rice Milk: A low-fat beverage made from brown rice. Rice milk is rich in complex carbohydrates and a good alternative to use in dairy- and soy-intolerant diets.

Rice Vinegar

Rice Vinegar: A mild, sweet vinegar made from rice. Excellent in salad dressings, marinades, and sauces.

Sea Salt

Sea Salt: Made by evaporating ocean water. Unlike table salt, sea salt is high in trace minerals and preferable as a seasoning.

Sesame Oil: Two types are available from roasted and unroasted sesame seeds. A delicate, brown oil is made from roasted sesame seeds. It adds a delicious aroma and flavor when added as a final seasoning to a cooked dish or dressing. The other type is a golden oil expressed from unroasted sesame seeds and used as an all-purpose vegetable oil. Our recipes call for the roasted, Chinese-style oil.

Sesame Oil

Silken Tofu: Silken tofu has a soft texture and is best used when a very creamy consistency is desired. This Japanese brand of tofu is often sold in unrefrigerated vacuum packages.

Silken Tofu

Shiitake: Large, full-flavored Japanese mushrooms. Shiitakes are said to boost the immune system. They are delicious in soups, sauces, and stir-fries and are available dried or fresh.

Shiitake

Soba Noodles: Japanese noodles made from buckwheat.

Soba Noodles

Soymilk: A non-dairy alternative to milk made from soybeans that have been soaked, finely ground with water, cooked, and strained. Soymilk can be found in unrefrigerated vacuum-packed cartons at health food stores and most supermarkets. There are a variety of flavors available. We recommend "plain" soymilk in our recipes unless indicated otherwise.

Soymilk

Tahini: A paste made from ground sesame seeds with a consistency similar to peanut butter. Used in spreads, sauces, salad dressings, and dips, tahini adds a rich flavor and essential minerals. We recommend the roasted variety.

Tahini

Tamari: Similar to soy sauce, but made by a slightly different fermenting process. Tamari may be used interchangeably with soy sauce.

Tamari

Tempeh: Cracked, whole soybeans that have been cooked, fermented, and steamed. Tempeh is packaged in square cakes with a variety of flavors and grain combinations. High in protein, tempeh is an excellent substitute for meat.

Tempeh

Tofu: Curd that results when ground soybeans are cooked, drained, and pressed into cubes. Tofu is low in calories, cholesterol-free, and abundant in protein, lysine, calcium, and iron, making it an essential component of the vegetarian diet. Because tofu is almost tasteless, it is amazingly versatile and can be seasoned and shaped into a variety of delicious foods. Fresh tofu is available in three textures—soft, medium, or firm. Fresh tofu is packaged in water; once opened, it needs to be stored in fresh water and rinsed daily.

Tofu

Tortilla

Tortilla: A thin, round, flat bread made from cornmeal or wheat flour. Tortillas are the national bread of Mexico and are cooked on a griddle with little or no oil.

Udon Noodles

Udon Noodles: A thick Japanese noodle made from whole wheat flour or brown rice.

Vine Leaves

Vine Leaves: The leaves of a particular grape vine used to make dolmades, a Mediterranean delicacy. Vine leaves are purchased in jars, preserved in salt water, and sold at Greek or Middle Eastern groceries or in supermarkets.

Yeast

Yeast: Yeast used for making bread comes in two forms: fresh (in a compressed cake) and dried (the form used in these recipes). Both varieties produce an enzyme which aerates the bread dough and causes it to rise.

BREAKFAST

Early morning hours at Shoshoni are a special time. A radiant sunrise lights the eastern sky as the cool mist lifts from the mountains. The surrounding valleys fill with the sweet melodies of our morning chant. After dawn meditation, resident yogis and guests eagerly file down to the dining hall for tea and breakfast. Shoshoni's morning staple is Indian Cereal, an ayurvedic recipe that prepares the body for the day. A bounty of fresh muffins, toasted homemade bread, and bowls of luscious fruits, granola, and yogurt are artistically arranged on the buffet table. Some days you will find a hearty mountain breakfast of Multi-Grain Flapjacks, Scrambled Tofu, or Golden-Baked Breakfast Potatoes. Begin your day with a sunrise meditation and one of our delicious breakfast recipes.

Banana French Toast

Yields 12 slices
PREP TIME: 15 minutes
COOKING TIME: 10 minutes

Start the morning with this easy-to-prepare, delicious French toast. It's especially good with Orange-Honey Syrup (page 29).

2 ripe bananas, sliced

3 cups soymilk or rice milk

½ teaspoon vanilla

1½ teaspoons cinnamon

2 teaspoons whole wheat flour

½ teaspoon salt

12 slices whole grain or French bread

1. Puree bananas, soymilk or rice milk, vanilla, cinnamon, flour, and salt in a blender until smooth and frothy.

2. Heat a griddle or skillet on medium, and brush lightly with oil. Test griddle with a few drops of water. Water should sizzle and evaporate, but oil should not smoke.

3. Dip bread slices into batter to coat evenly, and cook each on one side for 2 to 3 minutes. Flip bread over and cook the other side. Outer crust should be golden brown and a little crispy.

4. Serve hot off the griddle with Orange-Honey Syrup, pure maple syrup, or fruit jam.

Per slice: Calories: 109, Protein: 5 gm., Carbohydrates: 17 gm., Fat: 3 gm., Percentage of calories from fat: 25%

Blueberry Walnut Pancakes

Yields 1 dozen 4-inch pancakes
PREP TIME: 15 minutes
COOKING TIME: 15 minutes

These homemade cakes are filled with fruit, nuts, and whole grain goodness. Serve with Fresh Strawberry Syrup (page 29) or Orange-Honey Syrup (page 29).

1 cup whole wheat pastry flour

½ cup rolled oats

½ teaspoon salt

1 tablespoon baking powder

½ teaspoon cinnamon

1¾ cups soymilk or rice milk

1 tablespoon vegetable oil

1 cup fresh or frozen blueberries

2 ripe bananas, sliced

½ cup walnut pieces

1. In a large mixing bowl, combine flour, oats, salt, baking powder, and cinnamon.

2. Whip soymilk or rice milk and oil for 1 minute by hand or in a blender until frothy and light. Pour wet ingredients into flour and mix well. Stir in blueberries, bananas, and walnuts.

3. Preheat a lightly oiled griddle or skillet on medium until hot but not smoking.

4. Pour ¼ cup batter on the griddle. Cook about 3 minutes on the first side until bubbles form in center of cakes and bottoms are lightly browned. Turn and cook second side until lightly browned. If bubbles form before first side is brown, turn heat up slightly. If first side turns too dark before bubbles form, turn griddle down.

Per pancake: Calories: 122, Protein: 4 gm., Carbohydrates: 15 gm., Fat: 6 gm., Percentage of calories from fat: 44%

Breakfast Burritos

Serves 4
PREP TIME: 20 minutes
COOKING TIME: 20 minutes

Spice up your morning with these savory burritos. Wrap them "to go" for a breakfast on the run.

1 teaspoon olive oil

1 small onion, diced

3 tablespoons roasted green chilies, diced

½ cup tomatoes, chopped

2 medium potatoes, cooked, and chopped (to save time cook the night before)

1 pound soft tofu, mashed

½ teaspoon garlic powder

½ teaspoon oregano

½ teaspoon ground cumin

½ teaspoon turmeric

1 teaspoon salt

4 ounces Monterey Jack or Cheddar soy cheese, grated (optional)

4 large or 8 small whole wheat tortillas

½ cup Pico de Gallo (pg 93) or mild salsa

1. Heat oil in a skillet and sauté onions until translucent. Add green chilies, tomatoes, and potatoes, and sauté 5 minutes. Stir in mashed tofu, garlic, oregano, cumin, turmeric, and salt. Cook on low heat 5 minutes. Add grated cheese if used, cover, and set aside.

2. To warm tortillas, dry cook them in a skillet for a few minutes on each side.

3. Portion tofu-potato mixture according to number of tortillas, and spoon portions into the center of each tortilla. Spread 2 tablespoons salsa across filling. Fold in the edges and roll up burrito-style. Serve with additional salsa on the side.

Per serving: Calories: 310, Protein: 13 gm., Carbohydrates: 44 gm., Fat: 8 gm., Percentage of calories from fat: 23%

Brown Rice Pudding

Serves 4 to 6
PREP TIME: 20 minutes
COOKING TIME: 1 hour

This protein-rich pudding makes a wonderful breakfast or healthful dessert, and is a great way to use leftover rice.

1 cup soymilk or rice milk

1 cup soft tofu, cubed

2 ripe bananas, sliced

⅓ cup honey or brown rice syrup

½ teaspoon cardamom

½ teaspoon cinnamon

½ teaspoon salt

1 teaspoon vanilla

1 teaspoon fresh lemon juice

2 cups cooked short-grain brown rice

slivered almonds for garnish

1. Preheat oven to 350°F.

2. Blend soymilk or rice milk, tofu, bananas, and honey in a food processor until smooth. Add spices and salt, vanilla, lemon juice, and blend again.

3. In a large mixing bowl, combine tofu mixture with rice.

4. Spread pudding into an oiled 9" x 13" baking dish, and sprinkle with almonds. Bake for 1 hour or until firm and slightly browned on top.

Per serving: Calories: 252, Protein: 7 gm., Carbohydrates: 47 gm., Fat: 4 gm., Percentage of calories from fat: 14%

Fruit 'n Nut Granola

Yields 9 to 10 cups
PREP TIME: 10 minutes
COOKING TIME: 30 to 45 minutes

Wake up to this light, oil-free granola, sweetened with pure fruit juice. For a moist, chewy texture, bake granola for the shorter time. For a crunchier texture, bake longer.

4 cups rolled oats

½ cup sesame seeds

1 cup sunflower seeds

1 cup almonds, coarsely chopped

½ cup dried shredded coconut

1 cup wheat germ

2 teaspoons salt

1 (8-ounce) can frozen apple juice concentrate, thawed

½ teaspoon almond or maple extract

½ teaspoon ground cinnamom

1 cup dried date pieces

1. Preheat oven to 350°F.

2. In a large mixing bowl, combine oats, seeds, almonds, coconut, wheat germ, and salt.

3. In a small saucepan, bring apple juice concentrate, extract, and cinnamom to a boil, then remove from heat.

4. Pour warmed juice over dry ingredients, and mix well until evenly coated.

5. Spread mixture onto a cookie sheet, and bake 30 to 45 minutes, stirring every 10 minutes after the first 15 minutes.

6. Allow to cool. Stir in date pieces and store in an airtight container.

Per ½ cup serving: Calories: 298, Protein: 9 gm., Carbohydrates: 32 gm., Fat: 15 gm., Percentage of calories from fat: 45%

Golden-Baked Breakfast Potatoes

Serves 6 to 8
PREP TIME: 30 minutes
COOKING TIME: 20 minutes

This healthful alternative to fried potatoes has the crispy texture of hash browns without the extra oil. Serve them with Scrambled Tofu (page 28) and toast.

1 tablespoon olive oil

1 medium red or yellow onion, finely chopped

3 cloves garlic, minced

2 carrots, peeled and diced

4 russet potatoes, peeled and diced

½ cup water

1 red or green bell pepper, cut into ½-inch squares

1 medium yellow squash, diced

1 medium zucchini, diced

1 cup button mushrooms, sliced

½ cup shiitake mushrooms, sliced (optional)

2 teaspoons sea salt

½ teaspoon black pepper

3 tablespoons fresh parsley, minced

3 tablespoons fresh thyme, minced, or 1 teaspoon dried thyme

1. Heat olive oil in a large skillet. Add onions and garlic, and sauté, stirring frequently until soft and lightly browned. Add carrots, potatoes, and water. Cover and cook 10 to 15 minutes until potatoes are almost tender. Add peppers, squashes, mushrooms, and seasonings. Continue to cook uncovered, stirring occasionally 5 minutes.

2. Preheat broiler. Turn potatoes and vegetables into a lightly oiled, shallow baking dish, and broil 3 to 5 minutes until potatoes are browned.

3. If your oven doesn't have a broiler, bake at 475°F until browned.

Per serving: Calories: 112, Protein: 1 gm., Carbohydrates: 21 gm., Fat: 1 gm., Percentage of calories from fat: 8%

Indian Cereal

Serves 6
PREP TIME: 15 minutes
COOKING TIME: 10 minutes (cereal)

A Shoshoni staple, this ayurvedic recipe is said to warm the digestive system and prepare the body for the day.

OATS:

1 cup whole oats

1 teaspoon salt

5 cups water

6 to 8 tablespoons nutritional yeast (for topping)

MASALA:

1 medium onion

1 tomato

⅓ cup shredded coconut

½ cup water

2 tablespoons canola oil

2 teaspoons whole brown mustard seeds

1 teaspoon whole cumin seeds

½ teaspoon whole oregano seeds (optional)

½ teaspoon whole fenugreek seeds

½ teaspoon whole coriander seeds

1 teaspoon fresh gingerroot, minced, or ¼ teaspoon powdered ginger

½ teaspoon curry powder or garam masala (pg 15)

1. Add oats and salt to water, and cook to make a thin oatmeal.

2. In a separate pot, start masala by cooking onion, tomato, and coconut in ½ cup water for 10 minutes until tender.

3. In a small skillet, heat canola oil, add mustard seeds, and fry until they "pop." Add all other seeds and ginger, and continue frying over low heat until lightly browned. Stir in curry powder and remove from heat.

4. Add seeds to tomato-onion mixture, and puree in a food processor or blender until smooth.

5. Add masala to cereal and mix well.

6. Serve hot with 1 tablespoon nutritional yeast per bowl.

Per serving: Calories: 183, Protein: 6 gm., Carbohydrates: 15 gm., Fat: 11 gm., Percentage of calories from fat: 54%

Multi-Grain Flapjacks

Yields 1 dozen 4-inch pancakes
PREP TIME: 20 minutes
COOKING TIME: 15 to 20 minutes

These hearty, eggless pancakes are full of whole grain goodness. Serve with Orange-Honey Syrup (page 29), natural maple syrup, or your favorite fruit jam.

½ cup whole wheat flour

¼ cup unbleached white flour

¼ cup rye flour

¼ cup buckwheat flour

¼ cup cornmeal

½ teaspoon salt

1 tablespoon baking powder

1¾ cups soymilk or rice milk

1 tablespoon vegetable oil

1. In a large mixing bowl, combine flours, cornmeal, salt, and baking powder.

2. Whisk soymilk or rice milk and oil for 1 minute by hand or in a blender until frothy and light. Pour wet ingredients into dry mixture and mix well.

3. Preheat a lightly oiled griddle or skillet on medium until hot but not smoking.

4. Pour ¼ cup batter on the griddle. Cook about 3 minutes on the first side until bubbles form in center of cakes and bottoms are lightly browned. Turn and cook second side until lightly browned. If bubbles form before first side is brown, turn heat up slightly. If first side turns too dark before bubbles form, turn griddle down.

Per pancake: Calories: 73, Protein: 2 gm., Carbohydrates: 11 gm., Fat: 2 gm., Percentage of calories from fat: 25%

Scrambled Tofu

Serves 3 to 4
PREP TIME: 15 minutes
COOKING TIME: 15 minutes

Try these tofu "eggs" with whole grain toast or muffins for a high-protein breakfast without the cholesterol.

1 pound firm tofu

½ teaspoon vegetable oil

1 small onion, diced

½ cup mushrooms, sliced

½ cup green peppers, diced (optional)

½ teaspoon garlic powder,
   or 1 clove garlic, minced

½ teaspoon thyme

½ teaspoon curry powder

1 tablespoon tamari

½ teaspoon salt

pinch black pepper

¼ cup water

1. In small mixing bowl, mash tofu with a fork.

2. In skillet, heat oil and sauté onions until translucent.

3. Add mushrooms and green peppers, and sauté 5 minutes.

4. Stir in mashed tofu, seasonings, and water, and cook over low heat 3 to 5 minutes.

5. Adjust seasonings to taste.

Per serving: Calories: 141, Protein: 12 gm., Carbohydrates: 6 gm., Fat: 7 gm., Percentage of calories from fat: 45%

Orange-Honey Syrup

Serves 6 to 8
PREP TIME: 10 minutes
COOKING TIME: 10 minutes

A wonderful alternative to heavy, sweet syrups.

1 cup honey

½ cup orange juice concentrate

½ cup apple juice concentrate

2 tablespoons cornstarch

2 cups water

1 teaspoon cinnamon

1 orange, thinly sliced

1. In a heavy saucepan whisk together honey, juices, cornstarch, and water.

2. Bring to a boil; then reduce heat to low. Add cinnamon and orange slices. Simmer 5 minutes, stirring occasionally, until thick.

Per serving: Calories: 232, Protein: 1 gm., Carbohydrates: 57 gm., Fat: 0 gm., Percentage of calories from fat: 0%

Fresh Strawberry Syrup

Serves 4
PREP TIME: 10 minutes

This delicious topping for pancakes or french toast is a healthful alternative to processed syrups. Use frozen strawberries when fresh are not available.

2 cups strawberries, sliced

1 cup all-fruit strawberry jam

1 cup water

Puree 1 cup of strawberries with strawberry jam and water. Stir in remaining sliced berries. May be served warm or cold.

Per serving: Calories: 47, Protein: 0 gm., Carbohydrates: 11 gm., Fat: 0 gm., Percentage of calories from fat: 0%

APPETIZERS AND SNACKS

"Little knoshes," as we call them, are treats that make great finger food or additions to a meal. At Shoshoni, we celebrate special occasions, such as holidays, with a feast. The days prior to a "holy day" are spent in meditation practice and Seva (selfless service). During the Seva periods, people love to pack into the kitchen and work together on the meals and little knoshes. So whether you are preparing an elegant dinner party, a family holiday meal, or dinner date for two, try some of our little knoshes to make your meal a festive one.

Asparagus Spring Rolls

Serves 6 to 8
PREP TIME: 1 hour
COOKING TIME: 30 minutes

These light, delicious spring rolls are baked rather than fried to reduce fat content. Rolling spring rolls is done firmly yet gently to prevent tearing of the delicate filo pastry. Use Ginger-Tamari Sauce (page 79), or Tamari-Orange Dressing (page 104) as a dipping sauce.

4 cups green cabbage, shredded

1 carrot, grated

½ inch gingerroot, grated

1 tablespoon sesame oil

2 cups asparagus, tough ends removed and thinly sliced

1 cup broccoli, finely chopped

1 cup spinach, thinly sliced

6 scallions, thinly sliced

1 (1-pound) package filo pastry

1 tablespoon sesame seeds

sesame or canola oil for brushing filo pastry sheets

1. In a large pot, sauté cabbage, carrots, and ginger in sesame oil for 5 minutes. Add asparagus, broccoli, spinach, and scallions, and sauté 3 minutes. Stir frequently, but do not add water.

2. Transfer vegetables to a large bowl and cool. Drain excess liquid.

3. To make spring rolls, carefully unroll filo pastry sheets. Lay the stack of sheets flat on a work counter and cover completely with plastic to prevent drying. Place a large cutting board next to the stack, and place a single layer of filo on the board. Lightly brush with oil. Repeat with one more layer, covering the stack of filo again each time a sheet is removed. Cut through the two layers with a sharp knife lengthwise to produce two long strips.

4. Preheat oven to 375°F.

5. Spoon ⅓ cup filling onto the lower end of one strip. Fold the bottom end over the filling, then fold one inch of the outer edges in and continue to roll up the strip, tucking the edges in, to prevent leakage. Brush the outside lightly with sesame oil, and place on a lightly oiled cookie sheet. Continue making rolls until filling is used.

6. Sprinkle with sesame seeds and bake 20-25 minutes until golden.

Per serving: Calories: 241, Protein: 6 gm., Carbohydrates: 48 gm., Fat: 2 gm., Percentage of calories from fat: 7%

Dolmades
(Stuffed Grape Leaves)

Yields 30 to 35 dolmades
PREP TIME: 45 minutes
COOKING TIME: 1 ½ hours

These delectable stuffed grape leaves are often found marinated in olive oil, but this low-fat recipe uses very little oil. Dolmades can be served cold as an appetizer or heated with Fresh Tomato Sauce (page 78) as an entree.

2 cups water

1 tablespoon olive oil

⅓ cup pine nuts

1 cup white or brown basmati rice

⅓ cup currants

1 teaspoon dried dill

1 teaspoon dried oregano

1 teaspoon salt

¼ teaspoon black pepper

1 tablespoon tomato paste

2 (9-ounce) packets of vine leaves, or 1 large jar, packed in brine

juice of 2 lemons

1. Bring water to a boil.

2. In a large saucepan, heat oil. Add pine nuts and toast until golden. Add rice and stir-fry 2 minutes. Add boiling water, currants, dill, oregano, salt, and pepper. Return to a boil, stir, and reduce heat. Cover and simmer over low heat 20 minutes for white basmati rice and 50 minutes for brown basmati rice.

3. Stir tomato paste into cooked rice mixture. Transfer to a bowl and allow to cool.

4. If using dried vine leaves, place in a bowl and pour boiling water over them. Allow to soak 10 minutes. Drain and rinse with cold water.

5. To stuff leaves, open up a leaf and place 1 to 3 teaspoons of filling in the center of the leaf (amount of filling will depend on size of the leaf). Roll stem end of leaf up over filling, fold in sides and continue rolling into a tight, cylindrical shape, tucking in loose ends.

6. To cook, place torn or unused leaves in a large, heavy-bottomed pot. Layer stuffed leaves on top. Place plate on top of stuffed leaves, and add enough hot water to cover dolmades. Add lemon juice and cover pot. Simmer 1 hour. Allow to cool, then remove carefully and transfer to a plate or glass baking dish. Store covered.

Per dolmade: Calories: 39, Protein: 1 gm., Carbohydrates: 6 gm., Fat: 1 gm., Percentage of calories from fat: 23%

East Indian Cheewra

Yields 5 cups
PREP TIME: 15 minutes
COOK TIME: 30 minutes

Cheewra is a spicy, curried nut and grain party mix with an intriguing flavor.

1 tablespoon sea salt

1 teaspoon black mustard seed (optional)

1 teaspoon curry powder

½ teaspoon garlic powder

¼ teaspoon cayenne

¼ teaspoon nutmeg

¼ teaspoon black pepper

¼ teaspoon ground cloves

¼ teaspoon cinnamon

½ cup raw pumpkin seeds

½ cup raw whole almonds

½ cup raw whole peanuts

½ cup raw whole cashews

½ cup raw whole walnuts

2 cups puffed dry cereal

2 tablespoons canola oil

3-4 tablespoons honey

½ cup golden raisins

1. Mix spices in a small bowl.

2. Mix nuts, seeds, and cereal in a separate bowl.

3. Heat oil in a skillet, and add spices. Stir constantly for a minute until spices are lightly roasted. Add the honey and heat until bubbly.

4. Add nut mixture to the hot spices, and mix well, coating the nuts.

5. Preheat oven to 325°F.

6. Spread evenly on a cookie sheet, and bake for 25 to 30 minutes until golden brown. Stir occasionally.

7. Allow the nuts to cool before removing from cookie sheet and stir in raisins.

Note: To reduce the fat percentage by about 40 percent, replace almonds, peanuts, and walnuts with 1½ cups of chestnuts.

Per ¼ cup serving: Calories: 154, Protein: 4 gm., Carbohydrates: 11 gm., Fat: 10 gm., Percentage of calories from fat: 58%

Feta-Rolled Roasted Peppers

Yields 24 to 30 pepper rolls
PREP TIME: 30 minutes
COOKING TIME: 45 minutes

This colorful appetizer is a crowd-pleaser at parties. Use red, green, or yellow peppers to add a festive look to your holiday table. Drizzle with Sun-Dried Tomato Dressing (page 103).

4 red, green, or yellow bell peppers

1 recipe Tofu Feta (pg 107)

1. Wash peppers and pat dry. Place on a cookie sheet, and roast at 400°F for 45 minutes. Turn two or three times until evenly charred. The thin, paper-like outer skin will turn black and lift away from the flesh.

2. Wrap charred peppers in a damp towel until cool enough to handle. Carefully peel away charred skin, and rinse well. Remove stems and seeds, and cut peppers lengthwise into six to eight strips, about 1 ¼ inch wide. Trim to create a flat, smooth top edge.

3. Place pepper strips, outer side down, on a cutting board. Spoon 1 tablespoon of Tofu Feta onto the wider end of the pepper strip, and roll completely around cheese. Refrigerate until served.

4. Peppers may be eaten plain or drizzled with Sun-dried Tomato and Basil Dressing (page 103).

Per roll (without tomato dressing): Calories: 44, Protein: 3 gm., Carbohydrates: 2 gm., Fat: 2 gm., Percentage of calories from fat: 41%

Marinated Artichokes

Serves 4 to 6
PREP TIME: 45 minutes
COOKING TIME: 45 minutes

One of our favorite things about spring is the abundance of fresh artichokes. Try this delicious recipe as a special appetizer, salad, or party dish.

3 fresh whole artichokes

1 tablespoon olive oil

2 cloves fresh garlic, minced

1 cup white wine, optional

MARINADE:

½ cup tomato juice

3 tablespoons olive oil

juice of two lemons

2 cloves garlic, minced

3 tablespoons fresh parsley, minced

3 tablespoons fresh basil, minced

½ teaspoon salt

pinch black pepper

1. Trim artichokes by removing stalks and tough outer leaves. Trim barbs off the remaining leaves, and smooth artichoke bottoms with a knife. Brush bottom of the saucepan with olive oil, and sprinkle with minced garlic. Place artichokes, bottoms down, in the pot, and lightly brown the bottoms. Invert the artichokes and fill the pot with water or stock and white wine.

2. Cover and simmer 45 minutes or until a leaf pulls away easily and is tender to eat. Drain the artichokes, and chill. When thoroughly chilled, cut in quarters through the bottoms (hearts). Scrape out the chokes (fuzzy thistles).

3. In a small mixing bowl, combine tomato juice, olive oil, lemon juice, garlic, parsley, basil, salt, and pepper. Pour mixture over the chilled artichokes, and allow to marinate until serving.

Per serving: Calories: 205, Protein: 2 gm., Carbohydrates: 10 gm., Fat: 13 gm., Percentage of calories from fat: 57%

 Samosas

Yields 12 samosas
PREP TIME: 1 hour
COOKING TIME: 1 hour

Samosas are curried vegetable turnovers popular throughout India. Samosas are traditionally deep fried, but we enjoy a delicious baked version that's lower in fat.

DOUGH:

- **2 cups whole wheat flour**
- **¾ teaspoon salt**
- **2 tablespoons canola oil**
- **¾-1 cup warm water**

FILLING:

- **1 medium onion, minced**
- **2 tablespoons canola oil**
- **2 teaspoons cumin seeds**
- **½ banana pepper (medium hot), minced**
- **½ teaspoon turmeric**
- **½ teaspoon ground coriander**
- **4 potatoes, boiled, peeled, and mashed**
- **1½ cups frozen green peas, thawed**
- **1 teaspoon salt**

1. To prepare the dough, blend flour, salt, oil, and water in a mixer or by hand until dough forms a ball. Add more water as needed to form a dough the consistency of moist pie dough. Cover and allow dough to rest 30 minutes.

2. To prepare the filling, sauté onions in canola oil until soft. Add cumin seeds, pepper, turmeric, and coriander. Sauté until seeds turn golden. In a large mixing bowl, combine onion and spices with mashed potatoes, green peas, and salt.

3. Preheat oven to 375°F.

4. To assemble the samosas, shape dough into 12 small balls. On a flat, lightly floured surface, roll dough into flat circles, 4 to 5 inches in diameter and ¼ inch thick.

5. Spoon 4 tablespoons of filling into center of each circle and fold half of the circle over the filling, forming a half-circle shape. Pinch edges together and score gently with a fork along rounded edge. Be careful not to tear the dough or let filling seep out sides.

6. Place samosas on a lightly oiled cookie sheet, and bake 40 to 50 minutes until golden.

7. Serve hot with Date Chutney (page 91), or Coconut Mint Chutney (page 89).

Note: For a different taste, 1 head cauliflower may be substituted for the potatoes.

Per samosa: Calories: 166, Protein: 4 gm., Carbohydrates: 26 gm., Fat: 5 gm., Percentage of calories from fat: 27%

San Francisco Pot Stickers

Yields 36 pot stickers
PREP TIME: 45 minutes
COOKING TIME: 25 minutes

Oriental steamed dumplings are always a special treat. They are delicious as an appetizer or as an accompaniment to other Oriental dishes. Serve with Ginger-Tamari Sauce (page 79).

1 tablespoon fresh gingerroot, minced

1 clove garlic, minced

½ medium onion, minced

½ green pepper, minced

4-5 fresh shiitake mushrooms or soaked dried mushrooms, thinly sliced

1 cup Japanese or regular eggplant, minced

2 tablespoons tamari

½ cup water

1 package fresh wonton wrappers

1 tablespoon canola oil

1. Combine ginger, garlic, onion, green pepper, mushrooms, eggplant, tamari, and water in a skillet. Cover and cook slowly 15 minutes until tender. Thoroughly drain off excess liquid.

2. To assemble pot stickers, place a wonton wrapper on a flat working surface with one point facing away from you. Lightly moisten the two upper edges of wrapper. Spoon 1½ teaspoons of filling into center of wrapper, and fold bottom half up to upper half. Seal by gently pressing edges together. Cover a cookie sheet with plastic wrap, and place dumplings on sheet ½ inch apart until cooking time.

3. To steam, brush a non-stick pan with oil and heat over medium flame. When the pan is hot, place dumplings in the skillet and sizzle one minute on both sides to lightly brown. Add ¼ - ⅓ cup water, cover, and steam. Dumplings are done when water has cooked away (don't be alarmed if they stick—after all, that's where they get their name). Gently remove from the pan with a spatula.

Per pot sticker: Calories: 133, Protein: 1 gm., Carbohydrates: 5 gm., Fat: 1 gm., Percentage of calories from fat: 27%

Sautéed Cucumbers With Romaine

Serves 4 to 6
PREP TIME: 15 minutes
COOKING TIME: 5 minutes

Try this unusual salad as a first course to a special meal.

2 cucumbers

1 tablespoon sesame oil

2 tablespoons sunflower seeds

1 head Romaine lettuce, sliced in 1-inch strips

juice of one lemon

½ teaspoon dill

¼ teaspoon salt, to taste

pinch black pepper

1. To prepare cucumbers, peel, cut in half lengthwise, remove seeds, and chop in ¼ inch slices.

2. In a wok or wide skillet, heat sesame oil and lightly brown sunflower seeds. Add cucumbers and sauté 2 minutes until cucumbers start to turn clear.

3. Add Romaine and sauté until lettuce wilts. Remove from heat and toss with lemon juice, dill, salt, and pepper to taste. Serve immediately.

Per each: Calories: 68, Protein: 1 gm., Carbohydrates: 5 gm., Fat: 4 gm., Percentage of calories from fat: 53%

Silken Avocado Mousse

Serves 15 to 20
PREP TIME: 30 minutes (plus 4 hours refrigeration)
COOKING TIME: 5 minutes

A feast for the eyes and the palate, this creamy, dairy-free creation will bring rave reviews from your guests.
Serve with crackers and colorful raw vegetables.

2 cups water

3 tablespoons agar flakes

5 ripe avocados

¼ cup fresh lime juice

¼ cup salsa

2 teaspoons sea salt

1 tablespoon olive oil

1. Heat water in a small saucepan, and whisk in agar flakes. Bring to a boil, then lower heat and simmer for 3 to 4 minutes until agar is completely dissolved. Set aside.

2. Slice avocados into chunks and combine with lime juice in a bowl. Puree avocado, lime juice, salsa, and salt in a food processor until smooth.

3. Add agar solution and blend again until completely smooth.

4. Oil a non-stick, 6-cup mold. Pour mixture into mold and chill for at least 4 hours.

5. To unmold, set the mold in hot water for 1 minute. Cover the mold with a serving plate, and invert. Shake firmly to loosen, and lift the mold away from the mousse.

Per serving: Calories: 125, Protein: 1 gm., Carbohydrates: 8 gm., Fat: 10 gm., Percentage of calories from fat: 72%

SOUPS

Steaming, soothing, and satisfying, the allure of our home-made soups always draws a crowd to the Shoshoni kitchen. Most of us grew up on canned soups, but are ready to prepare and label our own inventions. Soup-making is easy. Prepared with goods on hand and mixed with a bit of ingenuity, a soup can become a wonderfully satisfying meal, on the table in a short amount of time. Important parts of the Shoshoni diet, soup, salad, and bread have been served together for years as a light, warming meal for lunch or dinner.

Apple-Beet Borscht

Serves 6 to 8
PREP TIME: 30 minutes
COOKING TIME: 2 to 3 hours

This lively version of traditional Russian beet borscht is delicious served hot or cold with a dollop of Tofu Sour Cream (page 108).

3 ounces tomato paste

4 cups water or light stock

¼ head medium red or green cabbage,
   thinly sliced

2 carrots, julienned

1 clove garlic, minced

3 beets, julienned

1 medium onion, thinly sliced

2 cups organic apple cider

¼ cup tamari

¼ cup sherry

2 tablespoons molasses, honey, or brown
   rice syrup

1 tablespoon dried dill,
   or 2 tablespoons fresh dill

2 teaspoons dried basil,
   or 2 tablespoons fresh basil

1 tablespoon caraway seeds,
   sautéed in 1 teaspoon canola oil

1. Combine all ingredients in a soup pot. Bring to a boil, then lower heat and simmer at least 2 to 3 hours.

2. Puree one-third of the soup; return puree to the pot and mix thoroughly.

Per serving: Calories: 105, Protein: 2 gm., Carbohydrates: 21 gm., Fat: 0 gm., Percentage of calories from fat: 0%

Ashram Lentil Soup

Serves 6 to 8
PREP TIME: 30 minutes
COOKING TIME: 1 hour

The aroma of this fragrant soup is sure to draw a hungry crowd to the table. Allow soup to sit for several hours or overnight for fuller flavor.

1¾ cups uncooked lentils

2 medium onions, chopped

2 cloves garlic, minced

4 carrots, sliced

1 teaspoon olive oil

1 tablespoon dried thyme

1 tablespoon dried basil

1 teaspoon dried oregano

8 cups water or stock

1 (1-pound) can of tomatoes, chopped or crushed

¼ teaspoon black pepper

2 teaspoons salt

1 cup fresh parsley, minced

¼ cup tamari

½ cup cooking sherry

1. Rinse lentils well. In a large soup pot, sauté onions, garlic, and carrots in oil until translucent. Add thyme, basil, and oregano for the last several minutes of sautéing.

2. Pour water or the stock, tomatoes, salt, pepper, and lentils into pot, and bring to a boil. Lower heat and simmer 45 minutes.

3. Add parsley, tamari, and sherry, and continue cooking for 15 minutes. Adjust seasonings to taste.

Per serving: Calories: 251, Protein: 13 gm., Carbohydrates: 42 gm., Fat: 1 gm., Percentage of calories from fat: 4%

Avocado Gazpacho

Serves 6 to 8
PREP TIME: 40 minutes

We took this classic chilled soup and added avocado for extra richness and a mellow, nutty flavor. Serve on hot summer days with Black Bean and Fresh Corn Summer Salad (page 62).

2 cups tomatoes, diced

1 small red onion, diced

1 cup green pepper, diced

1 cucumber, peeled, seeded, and diced

2 avocados, diced

2 scallions, minced

3 cups tomato juice

1 teaspoon honey

1 clove garlic, minced

1 tablespoon red wine vinegar

2 teaspoons salt

1. Combine all ingredients in a large soup pot or bowl.

2. Puree half the soup in a blender, return to the soup pot, and stir well to combine. Adjust seasonings to taste. Chill before serving.

Per serving: Calories: 144, Protein: 2 gm., Carbohydrates: 17 gm., Fat: 7 gm., Percentage of calories from fat: 44%

Carrot Mint Soup

Serves 4 to 6
PREP TIME: 20 minutes
COOKING TIME: 1 hour

A simple yet elegant soup with a creamy texture and natural sweetness.

6-8 carrots, peeled and chopped

1 medium onion, thinly sliced

3 cloves fresh garlic, minced

6 cups vegetable stock

2 teaspoons salt

½ teaspoon pepper

¼ cup fresh mint, chopped,
   or 2 teaspoons dried mint

2 tablespoons honey or brown rice syrup

1. Combine carrots, onion, garlic, and stock in a soup pot. Simmer 40 minutes or until carrots are very tender.

2. Remove carrots and puree with a little stock in blender until completely smooth. Return puree to the pot and stir well to combine.

3. Stir in salt, pepper, mint, and sweetener. Mix well and adjust seasonings to taste.

Per serving: Calories: 80, Protein: 1 gm., Carbohydrates: 19 gm., Fat: 0 gm., Percentage of calories from fat: 0%

Cauliflower And Squash Bisque

Serves 6 to 8
PREP TIME: 30 minutes
COOKING TIME: 45 minutes

This luscious soup is thick and satisfying, especially on cold winter nights.

½ cup onion, chopped

½ teaspoon olive oil

2 cups butternut squash, peeled and cubed

3 cups cauliflower florets

1 cup carrots, peeled and chopped

6 cups water or vegetable stock

⅓ cup rolled oats

½ teaspoon salt

pinch black pepper

pinch ground nutmeg

1. In a large soup pot, sauté onions in olive oil until translucent. Add squash, cauliflower, and carrots. Cook 5 minutes. Add stock, oats, and salt. Bring to a boil, then lower heat, cover and simmer 30 minutes.

2. Puree soup in a blender until creamy. Add more liquid if needed.

3. Before serving add pepper and nutmeg.

Per serving: Calories: 69, Protein: 2 gm., Carbohydrates: 14 gm., Fat: 0 gm., Percentage of calories from fat: 0%

Chili Corn Chowder

Serves 6 to 8
PREP TIME: 30 minutes
COOKING TIME: 45 minutes

Your family and friends won't believe there isn't heavy cream in this rich-tasting chowder.

2 medium onions

4 cloves garlic, minced

2 teaspoons olive oil

2 medium potatoes, peeled and diced

¼ cup celery, diced

¼ cup red bell pepper, diced

4 cups fresh or frozen corn kernels

¼ cup canned green chilies, diced

6 cups Light Vegetable Stock (pg 53)

½ cup white wine (optional)

1 teaspoon salt

½ teaspoon thyme

½ teaspoon sage

½ teaspoon chili powder

dash black pepper

1 cup silken tofu

1 tablespoon fresh lemon juice

¼ cup fresh parsley or cilantro, chopped

1. In a large soup pot, sauté onions and garlic in olive oil until translucent. Add potatoes, celery, and bell peppers, and sauté 5 minutes. Add corn and green chilies, and sauté 5 minutes. Add stock, wine, salt, thyme, sage, chili powder, and pepper. Bring to a boil, lower heat, and simmer for 30 minutes.

2. Puree ½ of the soup in a blender with silken tofu until completely smooth.

3. Return puree to the pot, stirring well to combine, and reheat on low. Before serving, add lemon juice and parsley or cilantro, and adjust seasonings to taste.

Per serving: Calories: 160, Protein: 5 gm., Carbohydrates: 28 gm., Fat: 2 gm., Percentage of calories from fat: 11%

Chilled Berry Soup

Serves 6 to 8
PREP TIME: 20 minutes
COOKING TIME: 20 minutes

This sweet, refreshing soup uses a variety of ripe, seasonal fruit. Serve as a first course in summer or as dessert any time of year.

1 tart green apple, peeled and diced

½ pound seedless red grapes

½ pound dark red cherries, pitted

1 cup water

½ cup dark grape juice

¼ cup pineapple juice

½ teaspoon grated orange rind

1 cup fresh strawberries, halved

1 cup fresh blueberries

1 cup fresh raspberries, blackberries, or boysenberries

2 teaspoons arrowroot powder

1 tablespoon apple juice

soy yogurt for garnish (optional)

fresh mint sprigs for garnish

1. In a large soup pot, combine apples, grapes, cherries, water, grape juice, pineapple juice and orange rind. Bring to a boil, reduce heat, and simmer 10 minutes until apples are tender. Stir occasionally.

2. Add berries and simmer 5 minutes.

3. Mix arrowroot with apple juice until completely dissolved, and stir into the soup. Bring to a boil, stirring constantly for 1 minute until soup thickens.

4. Chill and serve with a dollop of soy yogurt and fresh mint sprigs, if desired.

Per serving: Calories: 100, Protein: 1 gm., Carbohydrates: 23 gm., Fat: 0 gm., Percentage of calories from fat: 0%

Cream Of Asparagus And Mushroom Soup

Serves 6 to 8
PREP TIME: 20 minutes
COOKING TIME: 40 minutes

An elegant classic, this soup is a favorite in springtime.

1½ pounds fresh asparagus

1 cup mushrooms, sliced

½ cup onion, finely chopped

2 cloves garlic, minced

6 cups vegetable stock or water

½ cup unbleached white flour

6 ounces silken tofu

1 teaspoon salt, or to taste

1 teaspoon dried dill,
   or 1 tablespoon fresh dill

1 teaspoon dried basil,
   or 3 tablespoons fresh basil

pinch black pepper

1. Snap off tough ends of the asparagus spears, and discard. Cut off tips and set aside. Slice remaining stalks.

2. In a medium soup pot, combine sliced asparagus stalks, ¾ cup sliced mushrooms, onions, garlic, and ½ cup stock. Simmer 10 minutes until onions are translucent.

3. Slowly whisk in flour and continue to simmer 5 minutes, stirring occasionally until flour turns golden.

4. Whisk in remaining stock or water, and cook 15 minutes, whisking frequently.

5. Puree soup a little at a time, adding some tofu to each blenderful. Return to the pot and season with salt, dill, basil, and pepper. Simmer gently and add remaining mushrooms and asparagus tips. Simmer 5 minutes longer until asparagus tips are tender. Adjust seasoning before serving.

Per serving: Calories: 77, Protein: 4 gm., Carbohydrates: 12 gm., Fat: 1 gm., Percentage of calories from fat: 12%

Cream Of Butternut Squash Soup

Serves 8
PREP TIME: 30 minutes
COOKING TIME: 45 minutes

An all-time favorite recipe of Rudi's Restaurant in Boulder, Colorado. Simplicity is the real beauty of this naturally sweet and creamy soup. Always good for a first course or as a meal in itself with Honey Walnut Quick Bread (see page 179) and tossed salad.

1 medium butternut squash (approximately 4 pounds)

8 cups stock or water

1 medium onion, thinly sliced

1 clove garlic, minced

1 cup soymilk

3 tablespoons honey or brown rice syrup

1 teaspoon salt

 pinch black pepper

1. Trim ends from butternut squash; then peel, seed, and cut in large cubes.

2. In a large, heavy-bottomed soup pot, combine squash, stock, onions, and garlic. Bring to a boil and let simmer 30 to 45 minutes or until tender. Whisk with a wire whip, or puree half in a blender to break up most of the squash chunks. The soup will naturally thicken because of the starch in the squash.

3. Whisk in soymilk, honey, salt, and pepper. Adjust seasonings to taste.

Per serving: Calories: 132, Protein: 3 gm., Carbohydrates: 29 gm., Fat: 0 gm., Percentage of calories from fat: 0%

Creamy White Bean Soup
with Sesame Croutons

Serves 8 to 10
PREP TIME: 30 minutes
COOKING TIME: 2 hours

You can use any type of white bean to prepare this soup. The creamy, rich consistency is complemented by the savory crunch of homemade croutons.

3 cups dried white beans
12 cups water or stock
2-3 bay leaves
1 large onion, chopped
5 cloves garlic, minced
½ teaspoon thyme
½ teaspoon rosemary
1 teaspoon sage
1½ teaspoons salt
dash black pepper
1 tablespoon fresh lemon juice

FOR CROUTONS:

6 to 8 slices whole wheat bread, cubed
1 tablespoon olive oil
2 tablespoons sesame seeds
4 cloves fresh garlic, minced
1 teaspoon dried basil
½ teaspoon oregano
½ teaspoon thyme
1 teaspoon salt

1. Rinse beans and soak overnight. Drain and cook 2 hours in a large soup pot with water or stock and bay leaves.

2. After 1 hour add onions and garlic.

3. After 2 hours, when beans are soft, add thyme, rosemary, sage, salt, and pepper.

4. Puree soup in a blender until smooth and creamy. Return each blenderful back to the main pot, and keep warm until served.

5. Preheat oven to 350°F.

6. To make croutons, heat oil in a skillet and fry sesame seeds until golden. Add garlic and herbs, and sauté 2 minutes. Add bread cubes and coat with herbed sesame seeds. Spread croutons on a baking sheet and bake 15 minutes, stirring often.

7. Before serving, add lemon juice to the soup, and adjust seasonings. Serve with croutons.

Per serving: Calories: 320, Protein: 16 gm., Carbohydrates: 54 gm., Fat: 4 gm., Percentage of calories from fat: 11%

Fresh Tomato Soup
with Golden Saffron Rice

Serves 4 to 6
PREP TIME: 30 minutes
COOKING TIME: 1 hour

This soup is best made in the late summer when tomatoes are especially juicy and flavorful. The light miso helps reduce the acidity of the tomatoes and balances the flavors.

1 teaspoon olive oil

½ cup onion, chopped finely

4 cloves garlic, minced

4 cups fresh tomatoes, chopped small

1 (8-ounce) can of crushed tomatoes

3 cups vegetable stock or water

½ recipe Golden Saffron Rice (pg 159)

2 tablespoons light miso

**2 teaspoons fresh dill,
    or ½ teaspoon dried dill**

2 tablespoons tamari

½ teaspoon salt

1. Heat oil in a 3 to 4 quart soup pot. Sauté onions and garlic until translucent.

2. Add tomatoes and sauté for 5 minutes. Add stock. Cover and simmer for 45 minutes.

3. Add Golden Saffron Rice, miso, and seasonings. Let soup sit for 5 to 10 minutes to allow flavors to blend. Rice will expand as the soup sits.

Per serving: Calories: 158, Protein: 5 gm., Carbohydrates: 30 gm., Fat: 2 gm., Percentage of calories from fat: 11%

Hot 'n Sour Miso Soup

Serves 6 to 8
PREP TIME: 20 minutes
COOKING TIME: 30 minutes

A delightful twist on the traditional miso soup recipe. Serve with Sesame Soba Noodles (page 136) or your favorite stir-fry.

1 large onion, thinly sliced

3 quarter-sized slices of gingerroot, slivered

¼ cup tamari

2 tablespoons rice vinegar

2 medium carrots, sliced lengthwise

1 (6-inch) stick of kombu

8 cups water

½ pound firm tofu, cubed

3-4 tablespoons red miso

½ teaspoon black pepper

1. In a large soup pot, steam onions and ginger in ½ cup water until translucent. Add tamari, rice vinegar, carrots, kombu, tofu, and 8 cups water. Simmer gently 20 minutes until kombu is soft. Remove kombu, slice into thin strips, and return to the pot.

2. Before serving, remove 1 cup broth from the soup pot, and dissolve miso in broth, and return to the pot. Add pepper and stir well, but do not boil.

Per serving: Calories: 62, Protein: 4 gm., Carbohydrates: 7 gm., Fat: 1 gm., Percentage of calories from fat: 15%

Light Vegetable Stock

Yields 12 to 14 cups
PREP TIME: 15 minutes
COOKING TIME: 30 to 45 minutes

A light vegetable stock that can be easily prepared in advance and frozen for future use in your favorite soups.

6 stalks celery, coarsely chopped

3 carrots, coarsely chopped

1 medium onion, cubed

1 gallon water

Chop vegetables. Place in a heavy-bottomed pot with water. Bring to a boil and simmer 30 to 45 minutes or until vegetables have released their juices. Strain and use as needed. Stock will last one week in the refrigerator or can be frozen.

Per cup: Calories: 15, Protein: 0 gm., Carbohydrates: 3 gm., Fat: 0 gm., Percentage of calories from fat: 0%

Chilled Honeydew Lime Soup

Serves 4 to 6
PREP TIME: 15 minutes

A refreshing summertime soup.

1 honeydew melon, peeled, seeded, and chopped

⅓ cup fresh lime juice

1 cup apple juice

1 teaspoon fresh gingerroot, grated

½ lime, thinly sliced

4-6 fresh mint springs

Puree melon with lime, apple juice, and ginger. Transfer mixture to a serving bowl, and serve well chilled. Garnish each serving with a thin slice of lime and sprig of fresh mint.

Per serving: Calories: 75, Protein: 1 gm., Carbohydrates: 18 gm., Fat: 0 gm., Percentage of calories from fat: 0%

Mexican Corn Soup

Serves 6 to 8
PREP TIME: 20 minutes
COOKING TIME: 30 minutes

This simple-to-prepare soup always receives many compliments.

1 teaspoon olive oil

1 cup onions, finely chopped

2 tablespoons whole cumin seeds

8 cups corn, fresh or frozen

5 cups vegetable stock

1 tablespoon salt

pinch black pepper

6 tablespoon tomato paste

1 cup soymilk

½ teaspoon Tabasco sauce

½ bunch fresh cilantro, minced (optional)

1. In a large soup pot, heat oil. Add onion and cumin seeds, and cook for 5 minutes until onions are translucent. Add corn, stock, salt, pepper, and tomato paste. Simmer 25 minutes.

2. Puree half the soup in a blender, then return soup to the pot and stir well to combine. Add soymilk and Tabasco sauce, and reheat without boiling. Adjust seasonings to taste and add fresh cilantro, if desired.

Per serving: Calories: 190, Protein: 5 gm., Carbohydrates: 39 gm., Fat: 2 gm., Percentage of calories from fat: 9%

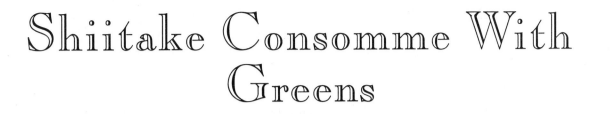

Shiitake Consomme With Greens

Serves 6
PREP TIME: 20 minutes
COOKING TIME: 30 minutes

A delicate soup that makes a great, light beginning to an elegant meal.

6 cups Light Vegetable Stock (page 53)

½ cup dried shiitake mushrooms (6 ounces fresh)

2 cloves garlic, minced

1 tablespoon sesame oil

1 pound greens (collard, mustard, or chard), chopped

1 tablespoon white miso

1 tablespoon lemon juice

dash black pepper, freshly ground

1. Heat stock in a large soup pot.

2. If using dried mushrooms, add them whole to the stock and simmer for 15 minutes. Remove with a slotted spoon. Cut off stems and thinly slice. If using fresh mushrooms, do not parboil.

3. In a skillet, sauté garlic and mushrooms in sesame oil for 4 minutes.

4. Add mushrooms and greens to stock, and simmer 15 minutes.

5. Before serving, dissolve miso and lemon juice in ½ cup soup stock. Add to soup but do not boil. Add freshly ground pepper.

Per serving: Calories: 52, Protein: 2 gm., Carbohydrates: 5 gm., Fat: 2 gm., Percentage of calories from fat: 35%

Tibetan Barley Soup

Serves 6 to 8
PREP TIME: 30 minutes
COOKING TIME: 2 hours

A simple, satisfying, and nourishing cold weather soup.

½ cup pearled barley

¼ cup lentils

6 cups stock or water

¼ cup celery, chopped

1 clove garlic, finely minced

1 medium potato, cut in ½-inch cubes

½ cup green cabbage

1 bay leaf

1 teaspoon sage

1 teaspoon whole rosemary leaves

1 teaspoon thyme

1 teaspoon salt

dash black pepper

2 tablespoons red miso

1. Rinse barley and lentils in cool water.

2. In a large soup pot, heat stock. Add barley and lentils, and cook on medium heat for 1 to 1 ½ hours until soft. Add vegetables and seasonings. Cook 20 minutes.

3. Before serving, dissolve miso in ½ cup soup stock. Add to the soup but do not boil.

Per serving: Calories: 77, Protein: 3 gm., Carbohydrates: 15 gm., Fat: 0 gm., Percentage of calories from fat: 0%

Tuscan White Bean And Tomato Soup

Serves 6 to 8
PREP TIME: 30 minutes
COOKING TIME: 2½ hours

This is a classic soup with a lovely blend of flavors.

1 cup dried navy beans (2 cups cooked)

8 cups water or stock

1 bay leaf

½ cup celery, finely chopped

1 teaspoon olive oil

½ cup onion, finely chopped

6 cloves garlic, minced

3 cups tomatoes (fresh or canned), chopped

2 teaspoons salt

3 tablespoons fresh sage,
    or 2 teaspoons dried sage

3 tablespoons fresh thyme,
    or 2 teaspoons dried thyme

¼ cup fresh parsley, minced

1. Sort beans and rinse well. Cover with cold water and soak overnight.

2. Drain off soaking water and transfer beans to a large, heavy pot.

3. Pour water or stock into the bean pot, and bring to a boil. Add bay leaf and chopped celery. Lower heat and simmer 2 hours.

4. Heat oil in a heavy skillet. Sauté onions and garlic until translucent. Add chopped tomatoes and simmer for 15 minutes.

5. When beans are fully cooked, add tomato mixture and seasonings. Simmer for another 30 minutes.

Per serving: Calories: 96, Protein: 4 gm., Carbohydrates: 17 gm., Fat: 1 gm., Percentage of calories from fat: 8%

Winter's Eve Potato Chowder

Serves 6 to 8
PREP TIME: 30 minutes
COOKING TIME: 45 minutes

5 medium potatoes, peeled and cubed

8 cups water or stock

½ teaspoon olive oil

¾ cup onion, chopped

5 cloves garlic, minced

¼ cup celery, chopped

3 bay leaves

1 teaspoon salt

½ teaspoon thyme

½ teaspoon tarragon

1 teaspoon sage

½ cup white wine

2 tablespoons roasted tahini

2 tablespoons fresh chives, chopped

dash black pepper

1. In a large soup pot, sauté onions and garlic in olive oil until translucent. Add celery, bay leaves, and salt. Cook for 2 minutes. Add stock, potatoes, thyme, tarragon, sage, and wine. Cook 30 to 40 minutes until potatoes are soft.

2. Puree half of the soup in a blender with the tahini.

3. Return to the pot, stir well to combine, and reheat on low. Before serving add pepper and chives.

Per serving: Calories: 129, Protein: 2 gm., Carbohydrates: 22 gm., Fat: 2 gm., Percentage of calories from fat: 16%

SALADS

A delightful way to enjoy the season's freshest fare, our salads range from simple, organic baby greens to hearty bean and grain affairs seasoned with fresh herbs and low-fat dressings. Salads inspire the imagination. A symphony of colors, textures, and flavors burst on the palate as well as the plate. The Ashram gardens give us the opportunity to cultivate a large variety of organic greens and herbs that add vitality to the Shoshoni salad bowl. When preparing salads at home, use the freshest ingredients. Prepare oil-free dressings by blending vegetables, such as sun-dried tomatoes or spinach, with water and herbs. For creamy dressings, add silken tofu.

Avocado Mint Salad

Serves 4 to 6
PREP TIME: 20 minutes

A refreshing tossed salad, perfect for warm summer days.

1 large avocado, cubed

1 tablespoon freshly squeezed lime juice

1 head bib lettuce, washed and torn

3 tablespoons fresh mint, minced

½ cup carrots, finely chopped or grated

½ cup fresh squeezed grapefruit juice

1 tablespoon sesame oil

1 teaspoon tamari

1 teaspoon apple juice concentrate

1. Toss avocado with lime juice.

2. Combine avocado, lettuce, mint, and carrots in a large salad bowl.

3. Blend grapefruit juice, sesame oil, tamari, and apple juice concentrate. Before serving, gently toss salad with dressing. Serve chilled.

Per serving: Calories: 131, Protein: 1 gm., Carbohydrates: 12 gm., Fat: 7 gm., Percentage of calories from fat: 48%

Beet Salad With Toasted Walnuts

Serves 6
PREP TIME: 45 minutes
COOKING TIME: 1 hour

This bright, colorful, and nutritious salad has created many loyal beet lovers. With its refreshing blend of natural sweetness, tang, and crunch, this salad is appealing any time of year.

1 pound whole beets with tops

1 medium red onion, very thinly sliced in half circles

1 cup walnuts, coarsely chopped and toasted

2 tablespoons balsamic or raspberry vinegar

2 tablespoons apple juice concentrate

3 tablespoons olive oil

1-2 teaspoons salt

⅓ cup fresh parsley, chopped

1. Wash beets well and trim off coarse tops, removing stems and greens. Save the greens.

2. Boil beets for approximately one hour until soft. Insert sharp knife into beet, and lift from the pot. Beets are ready when test beet drops easily away from the knife. Rinse in cold water. When cool enough to handle, peel off skins and cut beets into ¼-inch half circles.

3. Parboil onions until translucent.

4. While still somewhat warm, mix rest of ingredients and toss with beets and onions. Let stand at room temperature for at least 30 minutes. May be served slightly warm.

5. Trim greens from stems and serve as decorative green garnish around the salad.

Per serving: Calories: 228, Protein: 3 gm., Carbohydrates: 12 gm., Fat: 18 gm., Percentage of calories from fat: 71%

Black Bean And Fresh Corn Summer Salad

Serves 4 to 6
PREP TIME: 45 minutes
COOKING TIME: 2 hours

Summertime and the eatin' is easy! This high-protein salad is a refreshing summer main course. It's hearty enough to satisfy, yet has a light, bright taste that's perfect for warm days.

1 cup black beans, uncooked (2 cups, cooked)

1 tablespoon olive oil

1 tablespoon fresh lime juice

¼ cup picante sauce

½ teaspoon salt

½ teaspoon cumin, ground

½ teaspoon coriander, ground

¼ cup red onion, finely chopped

½ cup red pepper, finely chopped

2 scallions, finely chopped

½ cup celery, finely chopped

½ cup carrot, finely chopped

½ cup fresh or frozen corn kernels, cooked

½ avocado, chopped (optional)

2 tablespoons fresh cilantro, finely chopped

1. Sort and wash beans well. Soak in cold water overnight. Drain off soaking water.

2. Add beans to 6 cups fresh water, and bring to boil. Turn heat to medium-low and cover. Cook beans approximately 2 hours until tender. Do not overcook. Drain and rinse beans with cold water. Set aside.

3. In a small mixing bowl whisk, together olive oil, lime juice, picante, salt, cumin, and coriander.

4. In a larger serving bowl, place chopped vegetables and beans, and toss with dressing.

5. Add avocado just before serving, if desired, and garnish with cilantro.

Per serving: Calories: 145, Protein: 6 gm., Carbohydrates: 23 gm., Fat: 2 gm., Percentage of calories from fat: 12%

Broccoli Pepper Salad

Serves 4 to 6
PREP TIME: 25 minutes
COOKING TIME: 10 to 45 minutes

This light, flavorful salad adds color to any meal. Preparation is a snap if you use pre-roasted Italian red peppers.

2 red bell peppers,
   or 1 (6-ounce) jar of Italian roasted red peppers
1 bunch broccoli
1 tomato, chopped
½ cup yellow pear tomatoes, halved (optional)
1 teaspoon olive oil
1 tablespoon raspberry or balsamic vinegar
1 teaspoon Dijon-style mustard
1 tablespoon lemon juice
2 dashes Tabasco sauce
¼ cup fresh basil, chopped
2 tablespoons fresh chives, chopped
¼ teaspoon salt

1. If using fresh peppers, preheat oven to 400°F.

2. Roast by placing peppers on a cookie sheet and baking for 45 minutes. Turn two or three times while roasting until evenly charred. Wrap charred peppers in a damp towel until cool enough to handle. Carefully peel away charred skin, and rinse well to remove black flecks, stems, and seeds. Cut peppers lengthwise into thin strips.

3. To prepare broccoli, cut florets in even sizes. Remove hard end of stalk, and trim away tough outer skin of stalks. Slice stalks in thin diagonals. Steam broccoli for 3-5 minutes until bright green and slightly tender. Rinse with cold water.

4. Place tomatoes, broccoli, and peppers in a large mixing bowl.

5. Whisk together olive oil, vinegar, mustard, lemon juice, Tabasco sauce, basil, chives, and salt. Pour dressing over the vegetables, and toss well. Adjust seasonings and serve chilled or at room temperature.

Per serving: Calories: 45, Protein: 2 gm., Carbohydrates: 6 gm., Fat: 1 gm., Percentage of calories from fat: 20%

Brussels Sprouts Salad
with Mustard Dressing

Serves 4 to 6
PREP TIME: 15 minutes
COOKING TIME: 15 minutes

A tasty autumn salad with a warming, mildly spicy dressing.

4 cups brussels sprouts

4 tablespoons rice vinegar

1 tablespoon olive oil

1 tablespoon Dijon-style mustard

1 tablespoon apple juice concentrate

¼ teaspoon salt

1 cup alfalfa or radish sprouts

1. Trim ends from brussels sprouts, and cut lengthwise in halves or quarters.

2. Mix vinegar, oil, mustard, apple juice concentrate, and salt. Set aside for flavors to blend.

3. In medium pot, bring 6 cups water to boil. Add brussels sprouts and cook 15 minutes until tender. Drain well.

4. While brussels sprouts are still warm, toss with dressing and set aside to cool. Toss in alfalfa sprouts. Serve at room temperature on a bed of bib lettuce.

Per serving: Calories: 88, Protein: 2 gm., Carbohydrates: 12 gm., Fat: 4 gm., Percentage of calories from fat: 41%

Cucumber And White Radish Salad

Serves 4 to 6
PREP TIME: 20 minutes

2 medium cucumbers, peeled, seeded, and shredded

2 cups daikon (white radish), peeled and shredded

1 cup soy yogurt (pg 109)

salt to taste

2 teaspoons cumin seeds, roasted

2 tablespoons slivered almonds, toasted

2 tablespoons sesame seeds, roasted

1 tablespoon fresh mint, minced

Combine cucumbers, daikon, soy yogurt, salt, and cumin seeds in a bowl, and mix well. Transfer to a serving bowl. Garnish with almonds and sesame seeds, and sprinkle mint around edges. Serve chilled.

Per serving: Calories: 112, Protein: 4 gm., Carbohydrates: 14 gm., Fat: 5 gm., Percentage of calories from fat: 40%

Fragrant Rice Salad

Serves 6 to 8
PREP TIME: 25 minutes
COOKING TIME: 20 minutes (for the rice)

Sweet, delicate basmati rice is tossed with garden fresh vegetables and aromatic coriander in this light, luscious salad.

4 cups basmati rice, cooked
    (2 cups uncooked)

2 cups fresh spinach, washed, stems
    removed, and chopped

4 scallions, sliced

1 large vine-ripened tomato,
    or 6 soaked, sun-dried tomatoes,
    chopped

1 carrot, peeled and grated

1 teaspoon olive oil

1 clove garlic, minced

4 tablespoons tamari

4 tablespoons rice vinegar

1 teaspoon salt, to taste

½ teaspoon ground coriander

1. In a large salad bowl, combine cooked rice, spinach, scallions, tomatoes, and carrot.

2. Whisk together olive oil, garlic, tamari, vinegar, salt, and coriander.

3. Pour dressing over rice and toss well. Adjust seasonings to taste.

Per serving: Calories: 157, Protein: 4 gm., Carbohydrates: 32 gm., Fat: 1 gm., Percentage of calories from fat: 6%

Marinated Vegetable Salad

Serves 6
PREP TIME: 30 minutes
COOKING TIME: 15 minutes

This colorful combination of steamed vegetables and fresh herbs is a refreshing alternative to green salad anytime of year.

1 head cauliflower, separated into florets

2 carrots, cut into matchsticks

1 medium onion, minced

1 bunch broccoli, separated into florets

1 tablespoon fresh basil, minced,
   or 1 teaspoon dried

1 tablespoon fresh dill, minced,
   or 1 teaspoon dried

2 teaspoons caraway seeds, fried in
   1 tablespoon olive oil until brown

1 teaspoon salt

½ teaspoon black pepper

½ cup rice, balsamic, or raspberry vinegar

1 zucchini, grated

1. Steam cauliflower, carrots, and onion 8 to 10 minutes until tender. Steam broccoli 5 minutes until bright green and tender.

2. Mix herbs and seasonings with vinegar.

3. In a large bowl, toss cooked vegetables and grated zucchini with dressing, and chill.

Per serving: Calories: 54, Protein: 2 gm., Carbohydrates: 11 gm., Fat: 0 gm., Percentage of calories from fat: 0%

Oriental Slaw

Serves 4 to 6
PREP TIME: 20 minutes

This exotic salad is an easily made crowd-pleaser.

1 small head Chinese cabbage, finely chopped

2 cups red cabbage, finely chopped

1 bunch scallions , thinly sliced

2 tablespoons sesame oil

¼ cup rice vinegar

1 teaspoon salt

¼ teaspoon Chinese Five Spice Powder (pg 14)

2 teaspoons honey or brown rice syrup

1. Combine Chinese cabbage, red cabbage, and scallions.

2. Blend oil, vinegar, salt, spice powder, and honey or rice syrup.

3. Pour dressing over vegetables, mix well, and chill.

Per serving: Calories: 77, Protein: 1 gm., Carbohydrates: 6 gm., Fat: 5 gm., Percentage of calories from fat: 58%

Pleasing Pasta Salad

Serves 6 to 8
PREP TIME: 30 minutes
COOKING TIME: 15 minutes

A simple salad that is perfect with Carrot Mint Soup (page 44).

¼ cup balsamic vinegar

2 tablespoons olive oil

1 tablespoon Dijon-style mustard

½ teaspoon salt

pinch black pepper

¼ cup fresh basil, chopped

2 cloves fresh garlic, minced

1 pound pasta of your choice

2 cups broccoli florets

1 cup red peppers, julienned

½ cup sun-dried tomatoes, soaked in warm
water for 30 minutes, drained, and sliced

1. In a small bowl, combine vinegar, oil, mustard, salt, pepper, fresh basil, and garlic for dressing. Set aside.

2. Cook pasta al dente, drain, and cool by rinsing under cold water.

3. Steam broccoli for 5 minutes, drain, and cool.

4. In a large bowl, combine pasta, red peppers, tomatoes, and broccoli, and toss with dressing. Serve chilled or at room temperature.

Per serving: Calories: 131, Protein: 3 gm., Carbohydrates: 19 gm., Fat: 5 gm., Percentage of calories from fat: 34%

Shoshoni Potato Salad

Serves 6 to 8
PREP TIME: 30 minutes
COOKING TIME: 45 minutes

What's a summertime picnic without homemade potato salad? This light recipe features fresh herbs and vegetables.

6 red potatoes, boiled, chilled, and cut in chunks

2 carrots, sliced and steamed 8-10 minutes

1 head broccoli, cut in florets and steamed 5 minutes

1 small red or yellow onion, minced

3 tablespoons olive oil

½-¾ cup rice vinegar or raspberry vinegar

2 tablespoons wildflower honey

½ cup fresh herbs, (any combination of oregano, basil, summer savory, sage, dill, or tarragon)

2 teaspoons salt

¾ teaspoon pepper

1 teaspoon celery seed

1. In a large mixing bowl, combine potatoes, carrots, broccoli, and onion.

2. In a small bowl, whisk together oil, vinegar, honey, fresh herbs, and seasonings.

3. Toss dressing with vegetables and allow to chill before serving.

Per serving: Calories: 204, Protein: 3 gm., Carbohydrates: 36 gm., Fat: 6 gm., Percentage of calories from fat: 26%

Spicy Peanut Noodles

Serves 6 to 8
PREP TIME: 30 minutes
COOKING TIME: 6 to 8 minutes

This dish isn't low-fat, but our guests at Shoshoni love it so much we can't say no. High in protein, the nutty flavor makes it a delicious accompaniment to Empress Tofu (page 116).

1 pound Japanese udon noodles

1 tablespoon sesame oil

1 recipe Spicy Peanut Dressing (pg 102)

⅓ cup carrots, slivered

⅓ cup green onion, slivered

⅓ cup red bell peppers, slivered

3 tablespoons sesame seeds, roasted

1. Bring 12 cups water to boil in a large pot. Add udon noodles and cook 6 to 8 minutes until al dente. Drain and rinse with cold water. Toss noodles with sesame oil, and chill in a large mixing bowl.

2. When chilled, toss with Spicy Peanut Dressing, carrots, green onions, and red peppers. Garnish with toasted sesame seeds, and serve cold.

Per serving: Calories: 334, Protein: 11 gm., Carbohydrates: 25 gm., Fat: 21 gm., Percentage of calories from fat: 57%

Supergrain Salad

Serves 6
PREP TIME: 45 minutes
COOKING TIME: 25 minutes

Quinoa (pronounced keen-wa) is grown in the Andes Mountains, where it was once the staple food of South America. This ancient grain is now ironically called "the supergrain of the future" because of its nutritional quality. Quinoa (in a more complete balance than any other plant) provides all eight essential amino acids needed by the body to build protein. The grain is light with a distinctive, nutty flavor and is quick-cooking and versatile. Always rinse quinoa well before cooking.

1 cup uncooked quinoa

2 cups water

1 cup carrot, diced

2 scallions, sliced

½ cup celery, diced

½ cup red bell pepper, diced

½ cup toasted pumpkin seeds

¼ cup fresh lemon juice

3 tablespoons picante sauce

½ teaspoon salt

2 tablespoons tamari

1 clove garlic, minced

1. Rinse quinoa well. Put in a pot and dry roast over medium flame until grain turns golden brown and begins to pop. Stir frequently to roast evenly. Add water, bring to a boil, then cover and simmer 15 minutes until liquid is absorbed. Remove from heat and let stand 10 minutes.

2. Mix carrots, scallions, celery, peppers, and pumpkin seeds in a bowl. When quinoa has cooled, combine with vegetable mixture.

3. Whisk together lemon juice, picante, salt, tamari, and garlic, and toss dressing into other ingredients.

Per serving: Calories: 174, Protein: 8 gm., Carbohydrates: 24 gm., Fat: 6 gm., Percentage of calories from fat: 31%

Tabouli

Serves 6
PREP TIME: 25 minutes
COOKING TIME: 5 minutes

Tabouli, a Middle Eastern cracked wheat salad, has the distinctive flavor of fresh mint, lemon juice, and olive oil. Its flavor is best if allowed to sit for a few hours or overnight before serving.

1 cup fine bulgur (cracked wheat)

1½ cups water

1 bunch parsley, minced (1 cup)

2 tablespoons fresh mint, minced

juice of two lemons

2 tablespoons olive oil

2 cloves garlic, minced

2 teaspoons salt

½ bunch scallions, minced

2 tomatoes, finely chopped

½ cup carrots, grated

½ cup cauliflower florets,
    steamed (optional)

1. Bring water to a boil. Add bulgur, stir, cover, and remove from heat. Allow to sit 30 minutes until bulgur is tender. Spoon bulgur into a fine mesh strainer to remove excess liquid, then place in a bowl and allow to cool.

2. In a mixing bowl combine parsley, mint, lemon juice, olive oil, garlic, and salt. Add cooled bulgur and mix well. Stir in scallions, tomatoes, carrots, and cauliflower. Adjust seasonings to taste.

Per serving: Calories: 178, Protein: 5 gm., Carbohydrates: 29 gm., Fat: 5 gm., Percentage of calories from fat: 25%

Tempeh Almond Salad

Yields 2 cups
PREP TIME: 20 minutes
COOKING TIME: 25 minutes

This makes an excellent sandwich filling or a tasty salad when served on a bed of lettuce with fresh tomato wedges and raw veggies.

1 pound tempeh, thawed if frozen, cut in ½-inch cubes

½ cup water

¼ cup tamari

½ pound soft tofu

2 tablespoons lemon juice or vinegar

1 teaspoon salt

2 teaspoons Dijon-style mustard

½ teaspoon garlic powder

pinch black pepper

½ cup celery, diced

¼ cup red onion, minced

¼ cup carrot, diced

¼ cup slivered almonds, toasted

1. Steam tempeh in water and tamari for 25 minutes. Drain excess liquid and cool.

2. In a blender or food processor, blend tofu, lemon juice or vinegar, salt, mustard, garlic powder, and black pepper to the consistency of mayonnaise.

3. In a mixing bowl, combine cooked tempeh, celery, onion, carrot, and almonds. Stir in tofu dressing and adjust seasonings to taste.

Per ⅓ cup: Calories: 235, Protein: 17 gm., Carbohydrates: 18 gm., Fat: 10 gm., Percentage of calories from fat: 38%

Warm Spinach Salad
with Orange-Walnut Dressing

Serves 4 to 6
PREP TIME: 20 minutes
COOKING TIME: 5 minutes

This iron-rich salad is a zesty alternative to tossed lettuce. Prepare vegetables ahead of time, and toss in the hot ingredients just before serving.

1 pound fresh spinach, washed and chopped

juice from ½ lemon

1 teaspoon olive oil

2 cloves garlic, minced

2 small zucchini, julienned

¼ cup walnuts

1½ tablespoons orange juice concentrate

½ teaspoon salt

2 ounces Tofu Feta (pg 107)

1. Place spinach in a large salad bowl, and toss with lemon juice.

2. In a skillet, heat olive oil, and sauté garlic on medium heat for a few seconds. Add zucchini and walnuts, and sauté 3 minutes until walnuts are toasted. Add orange juice concentrate and salt.

3. Toss zucchini-walnut mixture into spinach, and crumble Tofu Feta over salad. Serve immediately.

Per serving: Calories: 101, Protein: 5 gm., Carbohydrates: 7 gm., Fat: 6 gm., Percentage of calories from fat: 59%

ACCOMPANIMENTS
Sauces, Dips, Relishes, Spice Mixes, Dressings

Hunger may be the best sauce, but we run a close second with our outrageous sauces, dips, dressings, and other accompaniments. Each sauce has a suggested use, so you can begin to explore their versatility and also create your own. Dips and dressings add a finishing touch to our vegetarian fare. Recipes like Hummus and Baba Ganouj inspire a meal in themselves.

Carrot Sauce

Yields 3½ cups
PREP TIME: 15 minutes
COOKING TIME: 10 minutes

Serve with Stuffed Swiss Chard (page 138) or Garden Style-Stuffed Potatoes (page 118).

2 cups carrots, chopped

1 clove garlic, minced

½ small onion, minced

1½ cups water

½ teaspoon salt

1. Cook all ingredients together 10 to 12 minutes until carrots are tender.

2. Puree mixture in a blender until smooth. Add more water for desired consistency.

Per ½ cup: Calories: 26, Protein: 0 gm., Carbohydrates: 6 gm., Fat: 0 gm., Percentage of calories from fat: 0%

Christmas Cranberry Glaze

Yields 4 cups
PREP TIME: 5 minutes
COOKING TIME: 10 minutes

Serve this tangy glaze with Royal Tofu Roulade (page 134) and Wild Rice Stuffing (page 163).

2 cups cranberry nectar frozen concentrate (for a less intense sauce, use cranberry juice instead of the frozen concentrate)

2 cups fruit-sweetened currant or cranberry jelly

1. Puree ingredients in a blender until they make a smooth sauce.

2. In a small saucepan, bring cranberry sauce to a boil. Lower heat and simmer for 5 minutes, stirring frequently, until sauce becomes a thick glaze.

Per ¼ cup: Calories: 100, Protein: 0 gm., Carbohydrates: 25 gm., Fat: 0 gm., Percentage of calories from fat: 0%

Fresh Tomato Sauce

Yields 6 to 8 cups
PREP TIME: 45 minutes
COOKING TIME: 30 minutes

Serve this sauce with Eggplant Rollatini (page 115), or Dolmades (page 32). When vine ripe tomatoes are available by the bushel, prepare a big batch of this fragrant sauce, and freeze it for the year. The fresh tomato flavor is much appreciated in the winter months.

1 medium onion, cut in half and thinly sliced

4 cloves garlic, minced

1 tablespoon olive oil

2½ pounds or 8 large tomatoes, sliced in wedges and seeded

1 stalk celery, thinly sliced

1 green pepper, seeds removed and thinly sliced

½ teaspoon salt

pinch black pepper

½ teaspoon dried basil, or 2 tablespoons fresh basil

¼ cup red wine

Sauté onion and garlic in olive oil until soft and translucent. Add tomatoes, celery, and green pepper. Cook briefly until vegetables are tender. Season with salt, pepper, basil, and wine. Let simmer 20 minutes for flavors to blend.

Per cup: Calories: 73, Protein: 1 gm., Carbohydrates: 9 gm., Fat: 2 gm., Percentage of calories from fat: 25%

Ginger-Tamari Sauce

Yields 1½ cups
PREP TIME: 15 minutes
COOKING TIME: 10 minutes

This makes a wonderful dipping sauce for Asparagus Spring Rolls (see page 31) and a basic Oriental sauce for Empress Tofu (see page 116) or San Francisco Pot Stickers (page 37).

1 tablespoon fresh gingerroot, grated

1 tablespoon fresh garlic, minced

4 drops sesame oil

½ cup tamari

1 cup water

4 tablespoons apple juice concentrate
   or honey

4 tablespoons rice vinegar

1 tablespoon agar flakes,
   or 1 tablespoon cornstarch dissolved in
   3 tablespoons cold water.

In a small saucepan, sauté ginger and garlic in sesame oil. Add tamari, water, apple juice concentrate or honey, vinegar, and agar or the cornstarch mixture. Bring to a boil, lower heat, and simmer 5 minutes. If you are using agar, the sauce will continue to thicken as it cools.

Per ¼ cup: Calories: 46, Protein: 2 gm., Carbohydrates: 9 gm., Fat: 0 gm., Percentage of calories from fat: 0%

Mom Putorti's Tomato Sauce

Yields 1½ gallons
PREP TIME: 30 minutes
COOKING TIME: 2½ hours

Swami Shambhavananda shares many colorful stories about his mother. After emigrating from Italy to Pennsylvania, she, Mr. Putorti, and their four sons managed a dairy farm and raised vegetables. Her spontaneous cooking style (using the day's pick for dinner) has always inspired us to use what we have on hand, and make it delicious. That's Italian! Serve this sauce with Eggplant Rollatini (page 115) or Tofu Lasagne (page 142).

1 #10 can of tomato sauce

2 medium onions, thinly sliced into half
    circles

¼ cup olive oil

1 eggplant, peeled and cut in thin
    1-inch strips

3 stalks celery, sliced

2 green peppers, thinly sliced

1 cup red wine

⅓ cup honey

¼ cup fresh basil,
    or 2 tablespoons dried basil

½ cup Italian parsley

1 tablespoon rosemary

salt and pepper to taste

1. Empty tomato sauce into heavy-bottomed pot. Fill empty tomato sauce can with water, and stir into sauce. Cook over low heat for several hours, stirring occasionally to prevent burning. Slow cooking develops a rich, full flavor while thickening the sauce.

2. Sauté onions in oil until translucent. Add other vegetables and sauté until tender.

3. Add sautéed vegetables to sauce at end of cooking time. Add wine, honey, and seasonings, and let sit for 15 minutes to enhance herb and vegetable flavors. Adjust seasonings.

Per cup: Calories: 103, Protein: 2 gm., Carbohydrates: 17 gm., Fat: 2 gm., Percentage of calories from fat: 17%

Putanesca Sauce

Serves 6 to 8
PREP TIME: 30 minutes
COOKING TIME: 1 hour

This sauce is great for adding to and using up whatever ingredients are available in your kitchen. We recommend that you follow this basic recipe first to get a feel for the sauce, then experiment with other ingredients next time. Serve over your favorite pasta, or use as a sauce for Eggplant Rollatini (page 115).

½ cup sun-dried tomatoes

3 cups water

1 tablespoon olive oil

1 medium onion, chopped

6 cloves fresh garlic, minced

1 small eggplant, diced

1 cup mushrooms, diced

½ cup tomato paste

3 cups diced tomatoes, canned or fresh

½ teaspoon oregano

1½ tablespoons salt

⅛-¼ teaspoon cayenne

pinch black pepper

3 tablespoons capers

¼ cup black olives, chopped

¼ cup fresh basil, chopped

1. Soak sun-dried tomatoes in 1 cup water for 30 minutes. Drain and thinly slice tomatoes, saving soaking liquid.

2. Heat olive oil in a saucepan. Add onions and sauté until translucent. Add garlic and eggplant, and sauté until soft. Add mushrooms and sliced sun-dried tomatoes, and sauté 3 minutes.

3. Stir in tomato paste and simmer 3 minutes. Add remaining 2 cups water plus the tomato soaking water, diced tomatoes, oregano, salt, cayenne, and pepper, and simmer over low heat 30 to 45 minutes.

4. Before serving, add capers, olives, and fresh basil. Adjust seasonings. Serve over pasta.

Per serving: Calories: 102, Protein: 2 gm., Carbohydrates: 16 gm., Fat: 2 gm., Percentage of calories from fat: 18%

Southwestern Sauce

Serves 4 to 6
PREP TIME: 30 minutes
COOKING TIME: 30 minutes

This versatile sauce is a complement to any Mexican or Southwestern dish, such as Black Bean-Avocado Enchiladas (page 112). Spice it up with more chilies if you prefer a hotter sauce.

½ cup almonds

5 cloves garlic, minced

1 jalapeño pepper, minced

1 medium red onion, minced

1 teaspoon olive oil

6 cups fresh or canned tomatoes, chopped

½ cup green chilies, diced

1 dried ancho red chile (optional)

1 cup water

½ teaspoon salt

1 teaspoon oregano

1 teaspoon cinnamon

2 teaspoons cumin

1. Preheat oven to 350°F.

2. Spread almonds on a cookie sheet, and roast for 15 minutes until lightly browned.

3. Sauté garlic, jalapeño pepper, and onion in olive oil until onion is golden. Add the tomatoes, chilies, water, salt, oregano, cinnamon, and cumin, and simmer for 10 minutes.

4. Puree the tomato sauce and almonds in a blender (2 cups at a time). Return to pot and simmer sauce for 10 more minutes.

Per serving: Calories: 145, Protein: 4 gm., Carbohydrates: 13 gm., Fat: 9 gm., Percentage of calories from fat: 55%

Tahini Sauce

Yields 2½ cups
PREP TIME: 15 minutes

This lovely sauce can be served over simple grains and vegetables or accompany sandwiches such as Fabulous Low-Fat Falafels (page 117), Vegetable-Tortilla Fold-ups (page 141), or Lakmajun (page 121).

1½ cups warm water

2 cloves garlic, minced

8 ounces roasted tahini

juice of one large lemon

¼ teaspoon ground coriander

¼ teaspoon ground cumin

1 teaspoon salt, to taste

pinch black pepper

3 dashes Tabasco sauce

Combine all ingredients in a blender, or whisk until smooth.

Per tablespoon: Calories: 34, Protein: 1 gm., Carbohydrates: 2 gm., Fat: 2 gm., Percentage of calories from fat: 50%

Zesty BBQ Sauce

Yields 2¼ cups
PREP TIME: 15 minutes

This sauce is great with Baked Marinated Tofu (page 106). Add to Pinto Beans (page 152) for old fashioned barbeque baked beans.

1 cup plain tomato sauce

¼ cup honey or apple juice concentrate

¼ cup soy sauce

¼ cup apple cider vinegar

1 tablespoon sesame oil

1½ tablespoons Dijon-style mustard

1 teaspoon basil, dried

¼ teaspoon ground cloves

¼ teaspoon ground ginger

⅓ cup onion, minced

¼ teaspoon cayenne

Combine all ingredients and allow to sit for 30 minutes.

Per ½ cup: Calories: 100, Protein: 2 gm., Carbohydrates: 21 gm., Fat: 1 gm., Percentage of calories from fat: 9%

Baba Ganouj

Yields 3 to 4 cups
PREP TIME: 20 minutes
COOKING TIME: 45 minutes

This is a Middle Eastern dip that everyone loves. Serve chilled or room temperature with raw vegetables, pita bread triangles, or your favorite whole grain crackers.

2 medium eggplants

½ cup tahini

3 medium cloves garlic, minced

½ cup parsley, chopped

1 teaspoon salt

juice from 2 large lemons

pinch black pepper

pinch cayenne

1. Preheat oven to 400°F.

2. Prick each eggplant about six times with a fork. Place directly on oven racks, and roast for 45 minutes. Remove and allow to cool. Cut off the stem ends, slice lengthwise in half, and scoop out the pulp.

3. Combine eggplant pulp with remaining ingredients; mash together well or puree in a food processor. Adjust seasonings to taste.

Per ¼ cup: Calories: 91, Protein: 2 gm., Carbohydrates: 9 gm., Fat: 5 gm., Percentage of calories from fat: 49%

Butternut Squash Spread

Yields 3 cups
PREP TIME: 20 minutes
COOKING TIME: 30 minutes

This delicious, low-fat spread makes the butter habit easy to break. Serve with whole grain breads, or use as a party dip with crackers and slices of French bread.

2 cups butternut squash, peeled, seeded, and cubed

½ cup onion, minced

1 clove garlic, minced

3 tablespoons almond butter

3 tablespoons white miso

1 teaspoon salt

1. Steam squash over boiling water for 25 to 30 minutes until soft. Drain well.

2. Sauté onion and garlic until translucent and slightly browned.

3. Blend squash, onion mixture, almond butter, miso, and salt in a food processor until creamy smooth. Adjust seasonings to taste.

Per 2 tablespoons: Calories: 90, Protein: 4 gm., Carbohydrates: 12 gm., Fat: 2 gm., Percentage of calories from fat: 20%

Guacamole

Yields 3 cups
PREP TIME: 15 minutes

Many people pride themselves on their favorite guacamole recipe. This one is simple and delicious. It's great with just chips or entrees such as Black Bean-Avocado Enchiladas (page 112), Blue Corn Empanadas (page 111), or Zucchini Pine-Nut Tamales (page 144).

3 ripe avocados, peeled and mashed

1 small red onion, minced and lightly sautéed

2 cloves garlic, minced and lightly sautéed

3 tablespoons fresh lime juice

1 jalapeño pepper, finely minced (optional)

¼ teaspoon salt

Combine all ingredients in a small bowl, and mix well. To prevent browning, store the guacamole in an airtight opaque container with an avocado pit placed in it until served.

Per ¼ cup: Calories: 88, Protein: 1 gm., Carbohydrates: 7 gm., Fat: 6 gm., Percentage of calories from fat: 60%

Hummus

Yields 4 cups
PREP TIME: 20 minutes
COOKING TIME: 2 hours

This Middle Eastern chick-pea and sesame paté has a spicy rich flavor and is full of protein. Use in pita pockets as a sandwich spread or as a dip with assorted raw vegetables.

1½ cups raw chick-peas, soaked overnight, or 3 cups cooked chick-peas

¾ cup tahini

3 medium cloves garlic, minced

¼ cup parsley, chopped

1 teaspoon salt

1 tablespoon tamari

juice from 2 large lemons

pinch black pepper

pinch cayenne

1. Drain soaking water from chick-peas. Boil in a large pot of water for 1½ to 2 hours until very tender. Drain cooking water.

2. Combine cooked chick-peas with all other ingredients in a food processor, and puree to a smooth paste, or mash chick-peas with a grinder or potato masher, and combine with other ingredients. Adjust seasonings to taste.

Per 2 tablespoons: Calories: 62, Protein: 2 gm., Carbohydrates: 6 gm., Fat: 2 gm., Percentage of calories from fat: 29%

Coconut Mint Chutney

Yields 1⅔ cups
PREP TIME: 20 minutes

Chutney is a sweet and sour condiment used with curried foods. This refreshing recipe is cooling and can be made hot or mild. Serve with Samosas (page 36).

1-2 jalapeño peppers, seeded and minced

1 tablespoon fresh gingerroot, grated

10 whole almonds, blanched

1½ tablespoons raw sugar or honey

⅓ cup fresh mint, chopped

⅓ cup fresh cilantro, chopped

1 cup fresh grated coconut with
    the coconut milk

juice of 1 fresh lime

soy yogurt (optional)

Place all ingredients in a blender or food processor, and grind until smooth. For a thinner dipping sauce, soy yogurt can be added. Chill until ready to use.

Per tablespoon: Calories: 64, Protein: 1 gm., Carbohydrates: 7 gm., Fat: 5 gm., Percentage of calories from fat: 54%

Cooling Soy Yogurt Raita

Yields 4 cups
PREP TIME: 20 minutes

Raita is traditionally served with hot curries to cool the palate. Serve this raita as a salad or condiment with Cauliflower Sabji (page 113), Sweet Corn and Coconut Curry (page 139), or Lentil Sambar (page 150).

2 cups soy yogurt

1 carrot, peeled and grated

1 small cucumber, peeled, seeded and thinly sliced

1 apple, peeled and thinly sliced

2 teaspoons fresh basil, minced

2 teaspoons fresh mint, minced

½ teaspoon salt

Combine all ingredients in a small bowl, and mix well.

Per ½ cup: Calories: 32, Protein: 2 gm., Carbohydrates: 4 gm., Fat: 1 gm., Percentage of calories from fat: 28%

Date Chutney

Yields 3½ to 4 cups
PREP TIME: 15 minutes
COOKING TIME: 15 minutes

This sweet chutney goes well with any curry. Serve with Masala Dosa (page 124) and Samosas (page 36).

1 pound dates, pitted and chopped

1 cup honey

1 cup vinegar

¾ cup water

3 cloves, garlic, minced

1 inch gingerroot, minced

½ teaspoon cumin seed

1 small green chili, minced

½ teaspoon salt

Combine all ingredients in a saucepan, bring to a boil, reduce heat to low, and simmer 10 to 15 minutes. Stir occasionally, making sure the chutney doesn't burn or stick on the bottom as it thickens. Store refrigerated in an airtight container.

Per tablespoon: Calories: 42, Protein: 0 gm., Carbohydrates: 11 gm., Fat: 0 gm., Percentage of calories from fat: 0%

Eggplant Tomato Relish

Yields 4½ cups
PREP TIME: 15 minutes
COOKING TIME: 1 to 1½ hours

This simple condiment can be served with rice or sandwiches such as Fabulous Low-Fat Falafels (page 117), Lakmajun (page 121), or Mudjedera (page 151).

1 medium eggplant, cut into ½-inch cubes

3 ounces tomato paste

1 medium onion, minced

4 cloves garlic, minced

2½ cups water

1 tablespoon basil

3 dashes Tabasco sauce

Combine all ingredients in a saucepan, and simmer on lowest heat for 1 to 1½ hours. Serve chilled or room temperature.

Per ½ cup: Calories: 31, Protein: 1 gm., Carbohydrates: 7 gm., Fat: 0 gm., Percentage of calories from fat: 0%

Pico De Gallo

Yields 2¼ cups
PREP TIME: 15 minutes

Oddly enough, Pico De Gallo means " beak of the rooster." While this wonderfully fresh salsa has nothing to do with roosters, it's certainly a "salsa" to crow about. Great with baked corn chips or as a condiment for Zucchini-Pine Nut Tamales (page 144), Blue Corn Empanadas (page 111), or Breakfast Burritos (page 22).

2 cups firm red tomatoes, finely diced

¾ cup red onion, finely diced

¼ cup fresh cilantro, minced

2 tablespoons fresh lime juice

1 fresh jalapeño pepper, minced

½ teaspoon salt

Combine all ingredients and let stand 30 minutes. Adjust seasonings to taste.

Per 2 tablespoons: Calories: 16, Protein: 0 gm., Carbohydrates: 3 gm., Fat: 0 gm., Percentage of calories from fat: 0%

Almond-Date Masala

Yields 3 to 4 cups
PREP TIME: 20 minutes
COOKING TIME: 1 hour

Masala is a mixture of spices, vegetables, fruits, and nuts that gives Indian food its unique flavor. This masala is slightly sweet and makes a delicious addition to vegetables or rice dishes such as Pumpkin and Green Pea Curry (page 131), Sweet Corn and Coconut Curry (page 139), or Mixed Vegetable Pulloa (page 125).

½ cup slivered almonds

1 tablespoon whole cumin seeds

1 tablespoon whole brown mustard seed

1 tablespoon oil

½ cup pitted dates

½ cup dal, red lentils, or yellow split peas

2 tomatoes, chopped

2 medium onions, chopped

1 teaspoon red chili paste,
    or ½ teaspoon cayenne

1 teaspoon salt

1 tablespoon fresh lemon juice

1 inch fresh gingerroot, grated

1. Sauté almonds and seeds in oil until browned.

2. Boil dates and dal in water until dal is tender. Drain well.

3. Puree all ingredients in a blender or food processor to make a smooth paste. Use to spice curries. May be frozen in small containers for future use.

Per ¼ cup: Calories: 103, Protein: 3 gm., Carbohydrates: 13 gm., Fat: 4 gm., Percentage of calories from fat: 35%

Mountain Masala

Yields 4 cups
PREP TIME: 20 minutes
COOKING TIME: 1 hour

Masala, a mixture of spices, vegetables, fruits, and nuts, gives Indian food its unique flavor. Curry powder, in fact, is simply a standard masala mix. You can replace curry powder or spice mixes in any traditional Indian dish with this exciting seasoning. Use in Masala Dosa (page 124) or Cauliflower Sabji (page 113).

2 medium onions, unpeeled and cut in half cross-wise

1 teaspoon canola oil

1 tablespoon whole brown mustard seeds

1 tablespoon whole cumin seeds

½ teaspoon cinnamon

½ teaspoon ground cardamom

1 teaspoon turmeric

½ teaspoon ground clove

½ teaspoon cayenne pepper

1 tablespoon coriander

1 inch fresh ginger, grated

3 cloves fresh garlic, minced

2 teaspoons salt

4 tomatoes, cut in wedges

1. Preheat oven to 375°F.

2. Place onions, cut side down, on a cookie sheet. Bake for 1 hour until caramelized. Onions will look charred and burnt on the outside, but will be golden and sweet on the inside. Discard roasted outer layer of onion.

3. Heat oil in a small skillet. When very hot, add brown mustard seeds and cumin seeds. Cover and lower heat until mustard seeds pop and turn light grey. Add remaining spices and stir.

4. In a blender or food processor, combine burnt onions, tomatoes, and spice mixture, and puree.

5. Use to spice curries. Masala also freezes well in small containers for future use.

Per cup: Calories: 60, Protein: 1 gm., Carbohydrates: 10 gm., Fat: 2 gm., Percentage of calories from fat: 30%

Celery Seed Dressing

Yields 4 cups
PREP TIME: 15 minutes

This sweet and tangy dressing is delicious on a fresh green salad or garden vegetables.

1 (10¼-ounce) package silken tofu, crumbled

2 cups water

⅔ cup apple cider vinegar or rice vinegar

3 tablespoons canola oil (optional)

¼ cup honey

¼ cup Dijon mustard

3 tablespoons celery seed

2 teaspoons salt

1 teaspoon fresh thyme or summer savory, minced

Combine all ingredients in a blender, and puree until smooth.

Per 2 tablespoons (with oil): Calories: 28, Protein: 1 gm., Carbohydrates: 2 gm., Fat: 2 gm.,
Percentage of calories from fat: 64%
Per 2 tablespoons (without oil): Calories: 17, Protein: 1 gm., Carbohydrates: 2 gm., Fat: 0 gm.,
Percentage of calories from fat: 0%

Creamy Ginger-Lime Dressing

Yields 2½ cups
PREP TIME: 15 minutes

A zesty complement to summer greens and fresh vegetables.

2 tablespoons fresh gingerroot, grated

2 limes, juiced

2 lemons, juiced

1 clove garlic, minced

2 tablespoons olive oil

2 (10¼-ounce) package silken tofu

3 tablespoons fresh basil, chopped

1 cup soymilk

½ teaspoon salt

pinch black pepper

Puree all ingredients in a blender, or whisk until smooth.

Per tablespoon: Calories: 18, Protein: 1 gm., Carbohydrates: 1 gm., Fat: 1 gm., Percentage of calories from fat: 50%

Fresh Basil-Garlic Dressing

Yields 2½ cups
PREP TIME: 15 minutes

Basil was once considered the "royal herb" in India where it was used as incense to purify temples. Nowadays, when the summertime brings us bunches of basil, we use it abundantly in pestos and dressings such as this one. Serve with Shoshoni Potato Salad (page 70).

3 cloves garlic, minced

½ cup fresh basil

½ cup balsamic vinegar

2 (10¼-ounce) packages silken tofu

¼ cup honey

1 teaspoon salt

1 cup water

Combine all ingredients in a blender, and puree until smooth.

Per 2 tablespoons: Calories: 37, Protein: 2 gm., Carbohydrates: 4 gm., Fat: 1 gm., Percentage of calories from fat: 24%

Garlic Journey Salad Dressing

Yields 2 cups
PREP TIME: 10 minutes

Flavors of fennel and ginger mingle with garlic to make this an unforgettable salad dressing.

3 cloves garlic

1 teaspoon fennel seed

½ teaspoon ground ginger

dash Tabasco sauce

¼ cup soy sauce

1½ cups water

¼ cup olive oil

2 red or green bell peppers, cut in chunks

1 teaspoon fresh parsley, finely chopped
   (optional)

Puree all ingredients in a blender. Chill before serving.

Per 2 tablespoons: Calories: 35, Protein: 0 gm., Carbohydrates: 1 gm., Fat: 2 gm., Percentage of calories from fat: 51%

Lemon Tahini Dressing

Yields 2½ cups
PREP TIME: 15 minutes

Dress up your summer greens with this refreshing, nutritious salad dressing.

1½ cups warm water

2 cloves garlic, minced

8 ounces roasted tahini

juice of one large lemon

2 tablespoons tamari

2 teaspoons cider vinegar

1 teaspoon basil

½ teaspoon ground coriander

¼ teaspoon ground cumin

1 teaspoon salt, to taste

pinch black pepper

3 dashes Tabasco sauce

Combine all ingredients in a blender, or whisk until smooth. Store refrigerated in a tightly covered jar.

Per tablespoon: Calories: 35, Protein: 1 gm., Carbohydrates: 2 gm., Fat: 2 gm., Percentage of calories from fat: 51%

Raspberry Poppy Seed Dressing

Yields 2½ cups
PREP TIME: 15 minutes

Raspberry vinegar is a wonderful condiment to have around the kitchen. It adds a fruity, sweet 'n' sour flavor to dressings, sauces, and soups.

½ cup raspberry vinegar

1 tablespoon Dijon mustard

⅓ cup apple juice concentrate

½ cup water

1 (10¼-ounce) block silken tofu

1 teaspoon salt

½ teaspoon dried rosemary,
    or 1 teaspoon fresh rosemary

1 teaspoon poppy seeds

pinch black pepper

Combine all ingredients and puree in a blender until smooth.

Per 2 tablespoons: Calories: 20, Protein: 1 gm., Carbohydrates: 2 gm., Fat: 0 gm., Percentage of calories from fat: 0%

Spicy Peanut Dressing

Yields 3 cups
PREP TIME: 15 minutes

Use this dressing with Spicy Peanut Noodles (page 71) or as a dip for raw vegetables. Also good with steamed vegetables and brown rice.

1 cup natural, unsalted peanut butter

2-3 cups water

1 tablespoon fresh gingerroot, grated

2 tablespoons rice vinegar

1 teaspoon salt

½ teaspoon Chinese red chili paste with garlic,
  or 2 cloves crushed garlic and ½ teaspoon crushed red chilies or cayenne

Puree all ingredients in a blender until smooth. Adjust seasonings to taste.

Per tablespoon: Calories: 32, Protein: 2 gm., Carbohydrates: 1 gm., Fat: 2 gm., Percentage of calories from fat: 56%

Sun-Dried Tomato And Basil Dressing

Yields 1½ cups
PREP TIME: 20 minutes

This tasty dressing complements Feta-Rolled Roasted Peppers (see page 34) and Polenta Torta (page 130).

¼ cup sun-dried tomatoes

1 cup warm water

¼ cup fresh basil, chopped

1 teaspoon salt

dash black pepper

1 tablespoon olive oil

1. Soak sun-dried tomatoes in warm water for 20 minutes until soft.

2. Combine all ingredients, including soaking water, in a blender, and puree until smooth.

Per ¼ cup: Calories: 37, Protein: 1 gm., Carbohydrates: 3 gm., Fat: 2 gm., Percentage of calories from fat: 49%

Tamari-Orange Dressing

Yields 1½ cups
PREP TIME: 10 minutes

This simple, oil-free dressing adds zest to your favorite garden greens and vegetables. It also makes a light dipping sauce for Asparagus Spring Rolls (page 31) or San Francisco Pot Stickers (page 37).

½ cup tamari

½ cup rice vinegar

½ cup fresh orange juice

1 clove garlic, minced

1½ teaspoons fresh gingerroot, minced

Combine all ingredients and blend well.

Per tablespoon: Calories: 7, Protein: 1 gm., Carbohydrates: 1 gm., Fat: 0 gm., Percentage of calories from fat: 0%

HEALTHFUL ALTERNATIVES

Tofu is the most versatile food on the planet. Its pure, white, soft form, without a strong taste of its own, lends itself to the chef's wildest creations. Better yet, it is high in protein and very low in calories, hence a good substitute for meats and cheese. Our Healthful Alternatives section gives some suggestions for using tofu to replace dairy ingredients in favorite recipes you want to adapt to a vegan diet.

Baked Marinated Tofu

Serves 3 to 4
PREP TIME: 10 minutes
COOKING TIME: 1 hour

This hearty tofu dish can be used as a sandwich filling or as a tasty addition to stir-fried vegetables.

½ cup water

¾ cup soy sauce

2 tablespoons sherry (optional)

2 tablespoons olive oil

2 tablespoons apple juice concentrate

¼ teaspoon dry mustard

¼ teaspoon cumin

½ teaspoon gingerroot, grated or ground

½ teaspoon garlic powder

1 pound firm tofu, sliced ¼ inch thick

1. Combine all ingredients except tofu in a container large enough to cover tofu. Cover with lid and shake.

2. Add tofu slices and marinate overnight.

3. To cook, preheat oven to 350°F.

4. Place tofu in a baking pan, and cover with marinade. Bake 45 minutes, turning tofu several times. Increase heat to 450°F and brown tofu for 5 to 10 minutes until slices turn crisp on the outside.

Per serving: Calories: 258, Protein: 17 gm., Carbohydrates: 12 gm., Fat: 15 gm., Percentage of calories from fat: 52%

Tofu Feta

Serves 4 to 6 (Yields 2 cups)
PREP TIME: 10 minutes

A low-fat substitute for recipes that call for Greek feta cheese.

1 pound firm tofu

1 teaspoon salt

1 teaspoon garlic powder

1 teaspoon olive oil

2 tablespoons lemon juice

1 tablespoon chives, minced

1 teaspoon dill, minced

Combine half of the tofu and all of the seasonings in a food processor, and blend until smooth. In a small bowl, mash remaining tofu with a fork, and stir in the blended tofu mixture. Adjust seasonings to taste and refrigerate.

Per serving: Calories: 78, Protein: 6 gm., Carbohydrates: 2 gm., Fat: 5 gm., Percentage of calories from fat: 58%

Tofu Ricotta

Serves 4 to 6
PREP TIME: 20 minutes

This creamy, dairy-free filling is low in fat and cholesterol.

1 pound firm tofu

1 teaspoon salt

1 teaspoon garlic powder

1 tablespoon fresh lemon juice

Combine half of the tofu and all other ingredients in a food processor, and blend until smooth. In a small bowl, mash remaining tofu with a fork, and stir in the blended tofu mixture.

Per serving: Calories: 70, Protein: 6 gm., Carbohydrates: 2 gm., Fat: 4 gm., Percentage of calories from fat: 51%

Tofu Sour Cream

Serves 4 to 6
PREP TIME: 10 minutes

Low-fat cuisine doesn't mean you have to give up rich, creamy favorites like sour cream topping on baked potatoes and tacos. Use extra silken tofu for a velvety-smooth consistency.

1 pound silken tofu

½ teaspoon salt

1 teaspoon garlic powder

2 tablespoons fresh lemon juice

1 teaspoon rice vinegar

Place all ingredients into a food processor, and blend until smooth.

Per serving: Calories: 71, Protein: 6 gm., Carbohydrates: 2 gm., Fat: 4 gm., Percentage of calories from fat: 51%

Soy Yogurt

Makes 1 quart
PREP TIME: 3 to 5 hours (includes setting time)
COOKING TIME: 10 minutes

Delicious soy yogurt can be made as easily as dairy yogurt. Be sure to use a good culture of either acidophilus or plain commercial yogurt made from milk, and make sure that the culture does not contain gelatin, stabilizers, or sugar.

1 quart plain soymilk

3-4 tablespoons plain yogurt

1. Heat soymilk to a temperature of 110°F (or warm to the touch).

2. Mix the yogurt culture with a small amount of warm soymilk, then add to the other milk.

3. Pour cultured soymilk into a sterilized glass jar, and cover. Set in a warm place, undisturbed, for 3 to 5 hours. If it does not set, the temperature of the soymilk may have been too high, and the culture was killed, or the place the jar was kept was not warm enough.

Helpful hints: Place the jar in a spot that will maintain a temperature of around 110°F. Try wrapping the jar with a blanket, and place in a warm spot in the kitchen, or set in an unlit oven, in a tub of warm water, or near a pilot light.

Per cup: Calories: 86, Protein: 6 gm., Carbohydrates: 5 gm., Fat: 5 gm., Percentage of calories from fat: 52%

ENTREES

As an Ashram community, we have scheduled meal times when everyone sits down together and shares a wonderful meal as a family (a custom lost in our society, with fast food and hectic schedules). Taking too many short cuts will compromise our health and humanity, so we believe in taking the time to create extraordinary entrees. A delicious meal prepared with love opens the hearts of those cooking and those partaking. Main courses at Shoshoni are a labor of love. Of course, busy schedules are inevitable, so we offer simple fare, like Sesame Soba Noodles or Vegetable Tortilla Fold-ups and range to extravagant dishes such as Royal Tofu Roulade and Polenta Torta.

Blue Corn Empanadas

Yields 12 empanadas
PREP TIME: 1½ hours
COOKING TIME: 1 to 1½ hours

Empanadas are savory, Mexican stuffed pastries. This recipe uses blue cornmeal and fresh vegetables for a highly nutritious and flavorful treat. The traditional method of preparation is deep frying. With this recipe, you have the option to fry or bake the empanadas.

2 cups blue cornmeal

1-2 cups water

2 cups unbleached white flour

⅓ cup soy yogurt (optional)

1 tablespoon canola oil

1 teaspoon salt

1 medium onion, finely chopped

1 red or green bell pepper, finely chopped

1 cup mushrooms, thinly sliced

1 cup cauliflower, finely chopped

1 cup broccoli, finely chopped

1 pound spinach, washed, steamed, and chopped

2 acorn squash or sweet potatoes, baked until soft, peeled and mashed

1 tablespoon whole cumin seeds

1 (6 ounce) jar (½ cup) Mexican green chili or tomatillo salsa

1 teaspoon salt

¼ teaspoon black pepper

Per each: Calories: 213, Protein: 6 gm., Carbohydrates: 43 gm., Fat: 2 gm., Percentage of calories from fat: 8%

1. To prepare dough, soak cornmeal in 1 cup water for 1 hour. Mix cornmeal, flour, soy yogurt if used, oil, and salt in a food processor or by hand until dough forms a ball, adding more water if necessary. The dough should have the consistency of moist pie dough. Cover and allow to rest 1 hour.

2. To prepare filling, steam onions and peppers until soft. Add mushrooms, cauliflower, and broccoli, and cook until vegetables are soft but not mushy. Mix in cooked spinach and mashed squash or sweet potatoes.

3. Roast cumin seeds in a few drops of oil until golden. Add cumin seeds, salsa, salt, and pepper to vegetables, and mix well. Set aside to cool. Adjust seasonings to taste.

4. To assemble empanadas, shape dough into 12 small balls. On a flat, lightly floured surface use a rolling pin to roll dough into flat circles the shape of small tortillas, 4 to 5 inches in diameter and ¼ inch thick.

6. Spoon 4 tablespoons of filling into center of each circle, and fold half of the circle over the filling, forming a half-moon shape. Pinch edges together and score gently with a fork along rounded edge. Be careful not to tear the dough or let the filling seep out sides.

7. To fry, heat 3 cups vegetable oil in a wok or small, heavy-bottomed pan until very hot but not smoking. Use a slotted spoon to place each empanada in the hot oil one at a time. Fry until golden brown, then drain on a paper towel, blotting excess oil.

8. To bake, place on a cookie sheet and bake 50 minutes at 350°F until golden.

9. Serve hot with Pico de Gallo (page 93) and Guacamole (page 87).

Black Bean~Avocado Enchiladas

Serves 6 to 8
PREP TIME: 1 hour
COOKING TIME: 1 to 3 hours

One of our most popular crowd-pleasers. For a fiesta meal, serve with Spanish rice, shredded lettuce, and Pico de Gallo (page 93).

3 cups dried black beans (6 cups cooked)

12 cups water

1 red onion, chopped (1 cup)

1 tablespoon garlic powder

2 teaspoons ground cumin

1 teaspoon chili powder

2 teaspoons salt

1 tablespoon lime juice

12 whole wheat tortillas

2 avocados, sliced into 24 strips

1 recipe Southwestern Sauce (pg 82)

1. Sort and wash beans well. Soak in cold water overnight. Drain off soaking water.

2. Add beans to 12 cups fresh water, and bring to boil. Turn heat to medium-low and cover pan. Cook beans approximately 2 hours until tender. Add more water as needed. Drain and rinse beans with cold water.

3. In a small skillet, sauté onions until translucent. Add garlic, cumin, chili powder, and salt. Stir spiced onions and lime juice into beans. Mash beans with a potato masher or blend in a food processor to desired consistency.

4. To assemble enchiladas, place tortillas on a flat surface. Spread ½ cup black beans down center, and place two strips of avocado over beans. Roll tortillas around beans.

5. Preheat oven to 375°F.

6. Spread one-third of the Southwestern Sauce on the bottom of 9" x 13" baking the pan. Place enchiladas in pan, side by side, and cover with remaining sauce. Cover pan with foil and bake for 45 minutes.

Per serving: Calories: 413, Protein: 13 gm., Carbohydrates: 55 gm., Fat: 16 gm., Percentage of calories from fat: 35%

Cauliflower Sabji

Serves 6
PREP TIME: 30 minutes
COOKING TIME: 35 to 45 minutes

Sabji is a "dry" vegetable curry. This mild curry is delicious combined with a spicy dal and basmati rice.

4 potatoes, peeled and cubed in ¼ inch pieces

1 tablespoon canola oil

2 teaspoons whole brown mustard seeds

1 tablespoon sesame seeds

2 teaspoons whole cumin seeds

6 cloves garlic, minced

1 teaspoon salt

3 cups cauliflower florets, sliced ¼ inch thick

1 cup tomatoes, chopped

¼ cup fresh cilantro, minced

1. Soak potatoes in cold water for half an hour.

2. Heat oil in a large, heavy sauce pan. Add mustard, sesame, and cumin seeds, cover, and sauté for a few seconds until they pop. Add garlic and salt.

3. Drain potatoes and add to sauté. Add 2 tablespoons water, stir, cover, and simmer 20 minutes until potatoes are tender. Add more water if needed.

4. Add cauliflower, tomatoes, and ½ cup water. Cover and simmer 10 more minutes until cauliflower is tender.

5. Allow liquid to cook off, remove from heat, and stir in cilantro before serving.

Per serving: Calories: 128, Protein: 2 gm., Carbohydrates: 23 gm., Fat: 3 gm., Percentage of calories from fat: 23%

Early Spring Primavera

Serves 6 to 8
PREP TIME: 45 minutes
COOKING TIME: 30 minutes

This pasta sauce uses pureed carrots instead of tomatoes for a luscious, slightly sweet, less acidic base. It's especially good in the springtime, prepared with fresh asparagus and snow peas, and served over colorful pasta spirals.

6 cups water

6 carrots, peeled and chopped

6 cloves garlic, minced

1 medium onion, finely sliced

1 teaspoon olive oil

½ cup red bell pepper, sliced

1 cup cauliflower florets

1 cup broccoli florets

1 cup mushrooms, sliced

½ cup artichoke hearts, quartered (optional)

1 cup asparagus, cut in 1 inch sections

2 teaspoons salt

⅛ teaspoon black pepper

¼ cup fresh basil, chopped

2 tablespoons fresh mint, chopped, or 1 teaspoon dried mint

½ cup snow peas

1. Bring 6 cups water to a boil. Cook carrots in boiling water for 15 to 20 minutes until tender. Drain carrots and set aside 2½ to 3 cups of the cooking water.

2. In a large skillet, sauté garlic and one of the onions in olive oil until golden. Spoon them into a blender, leaving any remaining oil in the pan for later.

3. Puree carrots, sautéed onions, garlic, and carrot water in a blender until very smooth. Set aside.

4. Use same skillet as in step 2 to sauté other vegetables until translucent—there should be enough oil left in the skillet. Add bell pepper, cauliflower, and ½ cup water; cover and steam 5 minutes. Add broccoli, mushrooms, artichoke hearts (if used), and asparagus; cover and steam 5 minutes. Add carrot puree, salt, pepper, basil, and mint; cover and simmer 5 more minutes. Add snow peas, cover, and simmer 1 minute.

5. Serve with colorful pasta spirals or linguini.

Per serving: Calories: 65, Protein: 2 gm., Carbohydrates: 12 gm., Fat: 0 gm., Percentage of calories from fat: 0%

Eggplant Rollatini

Serves 6
PREP TIME: 45 minutes
COOKING TIME: 45 minutes

2 medium eggplants

¾ cup flour

1 teaspoon dried basil

1 teaspoon powdered garlic

1 teaspoon salt

¼ teaspoon black pepper

3 tablespoons olive oil

FILLING:

4 cups Tofu Ricotta (pg 108)

¼ cup fresh basil, chopped

1 clove garlic, minced

pinch nutmeg

few dashes Tabasco sauce

1 recipe Fresh Tomato Sauce (pg 78)

6 scallions, minced

1. Peel and slice eggplants lengthwise in ¼ inch slices (12 slices total).

2. Prepare seasoned flour by mixing flour with basil, garlic, salt and pepper. Dredge eggplant slices in seasoned flour, and sauté in olive oil until browned and tender. Drain on a paper towel.

3. To prepare filling, combine tofu ricotta with fresh basil, garlic, nutmeg, and Tabasco sauce.

4. Preheat oven to 350°F.

5. Place ⅓ cup of the ricotta filling on each sautéed eggplant slice, and roll it up like a crepe. Place eggplant rolls in a deep baking dish. Cover with 6 cups of Fresh Tomato Sauce, and bake 30 to 40 minutes until bubbly and hot. Top with scallions and serve with additional sauce if desired.

Per serving: Calories: 361, Protein: 15 gm., Carbohydrates: 35 gm., Fat: 16 gm., Percentage of calories from fat: 40%

Empress Tofu

Serves 3 to 4
PREP TIME: 30 minutes
COOKING TIME: 15 minutes

A quick, delicious dinner served with brown rice and Spicy Peanut Noodles (page 71).

3 tablespoons olive oil

1 pound firm tofu, cut into ½-inch cubes or triangles

¾ cup carrots, julienned

½ cup red pepper, julienned

1 cup broccoli florets

1 recipe Ginger-Tamari Sauce (pg 79)*

*Substitute 2 teaspoons cornstarch mixed with 1 tablespoon cold water for agar in Ginger-Tamari Sauce recipe.

1. In a skillet, heat oil and fry tofu until crisp on the outside and soft inside. Remove tofu with a slotted spoon, and drain off excess oil with a paper towel.

2. Return tofu to the skillet, add carrots, red pepper, broccoli, and Ginger-Tamari Sauce. Cover and cook 5 minutes.

Per serving: Calories: 253, Protein: 12 gm., Carbohydrates: 17 gm., Fat: 14 gm., Percentage of calories from fat: 50%

Fabulous Low-Fat Falafel

Serves 8
PREP TIME: 30 minutes
COOKING TIME: 2 hours

These wonderful Middle Eastern chick-pea patties are lightly sautéed rather than deep fried. Serve in pita pockets with Tahini Sauce (page 83), Eggplant Tomato Relish (page 92), and lettuce leaves.

2 cups dried chick-peas (4 cups cooked)

1 cup wheat germ

1 onion, minced

4 cloves garlic, minced

1 bunch parsley, minced

1 teaspoon ground cumin

1 teaspoon ground coriander

⅛ teaspoon cayenne pepper

1 teaspoon salt or to taste

½ teaspoon baking powder

1 tablespoon olive oil

1. Soak chick-peas overnight. Drain off soaking water and cook in fresh water 2 hours until tender. Drain off cooking water and mash chick-peas well or puree in a food processor.

2. In a large bowl, combine mashed chick-peas and all other ingredients except oil.

3. Lightly brush a skillet with oil. Form chick-pea mixture into small patties 1½ inches in diameter, and sauté each patty on both sides until crisp on the outside.

Per serving: Calories: 211, Protein: 10 gm., Carbohydrates: 31 gm., Fat: 5 gm., Percentage of calories from fat: 21%

Garden-Style Stuffed Potatoes

Serves 6 to 8
PREP TIME: 45 minutes
COOKING TIME: 1½ to 2 hours

Each year these potatoes are requested by many of our returning retreat guests. They call for reservations and ask, "Can we have those yummy potatoes again?" A satisfying meal in themselves, these potatoes are especially good served with Tibetan Barley Soup (page 56) and a green salad.

4 large Russet potatoes, scrubbed

1 medium onion, chopped

1 teaspoon olive oil

4 cloves garlic, minced

2 tablespoons sunflower seeds

1 cup mushrooms, sliced

2 cups broccoli florets

2 teaspoons salt

½ teaspoon black pepper

¼ cup fresh basil, chopped

¼ cup scallions, chopped

1 teaspoon paprika

1. Preheat oven to 350°F.

2. Prick each potato with a fork a few times, and bake for 1 to 1½ hours until soft.

3. While potatoes are baking, sauté onions in olive oil until translucent. Add garlic, sunflower seeds, and mushrooms, and sauté 5 minutes. Add broccoli, cover, and steam 1 minute.

4. When potatoes are cool enough to handle, cut in half lengthwise and scoop out inner flesh, leaving skins as "boats" to be stuffed.

5. Bring oven back up to 350°F.

6. In a large mixing bowl, mash potatoes with a fork. Add sautéed vegetables, salt, pepper, and basil. Mix well and adjust seasonings to taste.

7. Spoon filling into potato skins, and pack firmly to form a rounded top. Place on a cookie sheet, and bake 20 minutes until hot.

8. Serve topped with scallions and dash of paprika.

Per ½ potato: Calories: 93, Protein: 2 gm., Carbohydrates: 17 gm., Fat: 2 gm., Percentage of calories from fat: 19%

Imam Bayeldi

Serves 8
PREP TIME: 45 minutes
COOKING TIME: 30 to 35 minutes

The Turkish name of this classic dish translates to "the priest fainted." According to Armenian legend, a housewife was surprised by a visit from a priest and, not having been able to prepare anything in advance, created this dish. At the first mouthful the priest fainted with delight.

4 small or 8 Japanese eggplants

3 medium onions, thinly sliced

1 tablespoon olive oil

1 green pepper, thinly sliced

4 cloves garlic, minced

6 tomatoes, peeled, seeded, and chopped

1 teaspoon salt, to taste

¼ teaspoon black pepper

½ cup fresh parsley, minced

¼ cup pine nuts (optional)

½ teaspoon coriander

fresh parsley or mint, minced, for topping

1. Place whole eggplants in a large pot, and cover with boiling water. Submerge eggplants with a heavy bowl or plate. Boil 15 to 20 minutes until tender. With a slotted spoon transfer eggplants to a pan of cold water to cool quickly.

2. Split eggplants in half lengthwise, score pulp, and remove without piercing shells. Set shells aside.

3. Sauté onions in olive oil until translucent. Add eggplant pulp and cook 10 minutes until tender. Add peppers, garlic, and tomatoes, and sauté for 5 minutes. Add salt, pepper, parsley, pine nuts (if used), and coriander, and adjust seasoning to taste.

4. To serve, fill shells with vegetables and sprinkle tops with fresh minced parsley or mint. Serve with Mudjedera (page 151) or couscous.

Per serving: Calories: 87 , Protein: 2 gm., Carbohydrates: 10 gm., Fat: 4 gm., Percentage of calories from fat: 41%

Kolokethopita

Yields 16
PREP TIME: 1 hour
COOKING TIME: 25 to 30 minutes

A perfect solution for those marathon zucchinis that fill the garden each summer.

8 cups zucchini, grated

1 bunch scallions, minced

3 cups cooked brown or basmati rice

1 pound soft tofu, mashed

2 tablespoons fresh basil, minced,
    or 1 teaspoon dried basil

½ bunch fresh parsley, minced

2 tablespoons fresh dill, minced,
    or 1 teaspoon dried dill

1 teaspoon salt

pinch black pepper

1 (1-pound) package filo dough

olive oil for brushing filo

1. In a large mixing bowl combine zucchini, scallions, rice, tofu, basil, parsley, dill, salt, and pepper.

2. To assemble Kolokethopita, carefully unroll the stack of pastry sheets. Lay them flat on a work counter, and cover with plastic to prevent drying. Prepare a large, clean surface next to the stack. Lay one sheet of pastry flat on the work surface. Use a soft pastry brush to lightly brush the sheet with olive oil. Use enough oil to barely moisten, but not saturate, the pastry sheets. Lay a second layer on top of the first, and again lightly brush with olive oil. Repeat with a third sheet.

3. Cut through the 3 layers lengthwise with a sharp knife to produce 2 long strips.

4. Preheat oven to 350°F.

5. Spoon ½ cup zucchini filling onto lower right-hand corner of one of the strips. Fold that corner up toward left hand edge to form a triangle, encasing the filling. Continue to roll up flag-style to the end of the strip until you have a triangular-shaped pastry. Brush the outside lightly with oil, and place on a cookie sheet. Continue to roll pastries until filling is used.

6. Bake for 25 to 30 minutes until golden.

Per triangle: Calories: 156, Protein: 5 gm., Carbohydrates: 30 gm., Fat: 2 gm., Percentage of calories from fat: 11%

Lakmajun

Serves 6 as entree
PREP TIME: 30 minutes
COOKING TIME: 1 hour

Lakmajun is a Middle Eastern pizza that can be prepared for lunch or cut in small wedges for an appetizer.

1 small eggplant

1 small onion, thinly sliced

1 teaspoon olive oil

1 green pepper, thinly sliced

2 tomatoes, minced

¼ pound mushrooms, sliced

4 cloves garlic, minced

½ teaspoon black pepper

1 teaspoon ground coriander

½ teaspoon cinnamon

2 teaspoons crushed basil

½ teaspoon salt

2 dashes Tabasco sauce

6 whole wheat pita

1 cup Tofu Feta (pg 107)

1. Preheat oven to 400°F.

2. Pierce eggplant about six times with a fork, and bake for 45 minutes until soft. When cool enough to handle, slit eggplant open and spoon out roasted pulp.

3. Sauté onions in oil until tender. Add eggplant and other vegetables, and cook until tender. Add seasonings.

4. Bring oven back to 400°F again.

5. Place pita on cookie sheet, pressing down centers and bringing up edges to form bowl shapes. Spread ½ cup of the vegetable mixture onto each pita. Top with even amounts of Tofu Feta.

6. Bake for 15 minutes. Serve cut in halves as a lunch, or cut into wedges for an appetizer.

Per serving: Calories: 222, Protein: 10 gm., Carbohydrates: 34 gm., Fat: 4 gm., Percentage of calories from fat: 16%

Layered Vegetable Bake

Serves 12
PREP TIME: 1 hour
COOKING TIME: 1½ to 2 hours

A distinctive casserole that presents a beautiful strata of colors, textures, and flavors.

LAYER 1:
   2 cups cornmeal
   ½ medium onion, minced
   3 cloves garlic, minced
   4 cups water
   1 tablespoon dried basil
   1 teaspoon salt
   pinch black pepper

LAYER 2:
   2 cups dried lentils
   ½ medium onion, minced
   3 cloves garlic, minced
   ½ teaspoon salt
   6 cups water

LAYER 3:
   1 medium onion, thinly sliced
   ½ pound mushrooms, sliced
   4 carrots, sliced
   ½ cup water
   1 green pepper, roasted and chopped
   2 yellow squash, sliced
   1 cup broccoli florets

LAYER 4:
   6 potatoes, boiled and mashed
   1 tablespoon caraway
   2 tablespoons fresh basil, chopped
   1 teaspoon salt
   pinch black pepper
   2 cups raw spinach or chard, chopped

1. Combine Layer 1 ingredients and cook on low for 20 minutes until water is absorbed and cornmeal thickens. Stir often to prevent sticking. Adjust seasonings.

2. Combine Layer 2 ingredients and cook 45 minutes until lentils are soft. Drain off excess liquid.

3. For Layer 3, steam onions, mushrooms, and carrots, in water until onions are soft. Add pepper, squash, and broccoli, and steam until broccoli turns bright green. Drain off excess liquid.

4. For Layer 4, combine mashed potatoes with seasonings and greens.

5. Preheat oven to 350°F.

6. To assemble casserole, spread cornmeal layer on the bottom of a 9" x 13" baking dish, and spoon lentil layer over the cornmeal mixture. Next, layer vegetables over lentils. For the top crust spread potato mixture over vegetables.

7. Cover with foil and bake for 45 minutes to 1 hour or until heated through.

Per serving: Calories: 260, Protein: 9 gm., Carbohydrates: 53 gm., Fat: 0 gm., Percentage of calories from fat: 0%

Mandarin Tofu

Serves 3 to 4
PREP TIME: 20 minutes
COOKING TIME: 35 to 50 minutes

An elegant entree that's perfect for a special dinner. Timing is the trick, so have all the ingredients ready and hot at the same time.

1 pound firm tofu, cut into ¼ inch slices

4 tablespoons tamari

4 tablespoons water

4 tablespoons sherry (optional)

1 teaspoon fresh gingerroot, grated

1 teaspoon fresh garlic, minced

2 cups freshly squeezed orange juice

½ cup white miso

½ cup tahini

½ cup carrots, julienned

½ cup broccoli florets

2 tablespoons scallions, slivered

4 tablespoons slivered almonds, toasted

1 (11 ounce) can mandarin orange slices

1. Place tofu slices on a cookie sheet, cover with plastic, and freeze at least 3 hours or overnight.

2. Preheat oven to 375°F.

3. Combine tamari, water, sherry, ginger, and garlic for marinade.

4. Remove tofu from freezer, brush with marinade, and bake 30 to 45 minutes until outer edges are browned.

5. For sauce, blend orange juice, miso, and tahini in a blender until smooth. Slowly heat in a small saucepan, but do not boil.

6. Steam carrots 5 minutes. Remove with a slotted spoon and keep warm.

7. Steam broccoli 3 minutes. Remove with a slotted spoon and keep warm.

8. Arrange tofu in the center of a large serving platter. Arrange broccoli around the tofu and the carrots around the broccoli. Drizzle with orange sauce and garnish with scallions, almonds, and mandarin oranges.

Per serving: Calories: 609, Protein: 22 gm., Carbohydrates: 56 gm., Fat: 31 gm., Percentage of calories from fat: 46%

Masala Dosa

Serves 6
PREP TIME: 1 hour
COOKING TIME: 1 hour

Masala Dosa is an all-time favorite at Rudi's Restaurant in Boulder. This rendition of an Indian classic is a spicy medley of curried vegetables wrapped in Brown Rice Crepes (page 157). Serve with Date Chutney (page 91) or Coconut Mint Chutney (page 89). See photo on front cover.

1 onion, diced

1 carrot, peeled and sliced

1 green pepper, chopped

3 cups broccoli florets

3 cups cauliflower florets

3 potatoes, boiled and peeled

1 tablespoon canola oil

2 tablespoons whole black mustard seeds

2 tablespoons whole cumin seeds

1 tablespoon fresh gingerroot, minced

1 tablespoon ground cumin

½ teaspoon turmeric

2 teaspoons coriander

½ teaspoon cayenne

2 teaspoons cardamom

pinch asafetida (optional)

1 cup frozen green peas, thawed

2 teaspoons salt

1 tablespoon fresh cilantro, minced

1 recipe Brown Rice Crepes (pg 157)

1. In a heavy-bottomed pot, steam onion, carrot, green pepper, broccoli, and cauliflower until tender. Mash boiled potatoes and add to vegetables.

2. In a small skillet, heat oil on medium flame and add mustard seeds. When seeds begin to pop, add cumin seeds and ginger. When cumin seeds turn golden, add ground cumin, turmeric, coriander, cayenne, cardamom, and asafetida. Fry spices while stirring for 1 minute.

3. Pour spice mixture over vegetables, and mix well. Stir in green peas, salt, and cilantro. Adjust spices.

4. Fold ½ cup vegetable filling into each brown rice crepe just before serving.

Per serving: Calories: 236, Protein: 6 gm., Carbohydrates: 46 gm., Fat: 2 gm., Percentage of calories from fat: 8%

Mixed Vegetable Pullao

Serves 6 to 8
PREP TIME: 30 minutes
COOKING TIME: 45 minutes

This traditional Indian dish, decorated with fresh vegetables and laced with aromatic spices, is a festive main course. Serve with Split Pea Dal (page 155) and Cooling Soy Yogurt Raita (page 90).

1 teaspoon olive oil

1 teaspoon cumin seeds

½ teaspoon turmeric

1-inch cinnamon stick

2 whole cloves

1 teaspoon chili powder

1 clove garlic, crushed

2 medium onions, thinly sliced

2 carrots, julienned

1 cup green beans, trimmed and sliced

½ cup red or green bell pepper, thinly sliced

1 potato, peeled and cubed

1 cup cauliflower florets

2 cups basmati rice, uncooked

4 cups hot water

1½ teaspoons salt

½ cup frozen peas, thawed

1 tomato, cut in wedges

¼ cup fresh cilantro, chopped

1. Heat oil in a skillet. When oil is hot, add cumin seeds, turmeric, cinnamon, cloves, chili powder, garlic, and onions. Fry for 3 minutes.

2. Add all vegetables and sauté 3 minutes longer on medium heat.

3. Add rice and sauté 5 minutes. Add water and salt, and bring to a boil.

4. When boiling, stir once, then lower heat, and cover. Simmer on low 20 minutes without stirring.

5. Allow to sit 5 minutes. Before serving, remove the whole spices that surfaced to the top, stir in the green peas and garnish with tomato wedges and cilantro.

Per serving: Calories: 191, Protein: 5 gm., Carbohydrates: 41 gm., Fat: 0 gm., Percentage of calories from fat: 0%

Moroccan Vegetable Tagine

Serves 6
PREP TIME: 45 minutes
COOKING TIME: 30 minutes

This aromatically spiced vegetable sauté is simple to prepare, yet gives the impression of a complex feast when served with couscous or Mudjedera (page 151)

1 medium onion, minced

1 clove garlic, minced

1 teaspoon olive oil

1 cup butternut squash, peeled and cubed

1 cup eggplant, peeled and cubed

1 carrot, cubed

½ cup water

1 cup cauliflower florets

1 medium-large zucchini, cubed

3 tomatoes, cut into wedges

½ pound fresh mushrooms, quartered

2 stalks celery, cut in half-inch slices

1 green pepper, cubed

½ cup cooked chick-peas

1 tablespoon fresh parsley, minced

1 teaspoon garlic

1 teaspoon basil

1 teaspoon cinnamon

1 teaspoon cumin

¼ teaspoon cayenne

1 teaspoon coriander

2 tablespoons fresh lemon juice

2 oz. (½ cup) figs or dates, chopped
salt to taste

1. Sauté onions and garlic in 1 teaspoon olive oil until clear and tender. Add butternut squash, eggplant, carrots, and water. Cook until tender, about 15 minutes.

2. Add cauliflower, zucchini, tomatoes, mushrooms, celery, green peppers, and chick-peas. Sauté until vegetables are tender and juicy, but not overcooked.

3. Add seasonings and figs or dates. Let stand 10 minutes for flavors to blend.

Per serving: Calories: 134, Protein: 3 gm., Carbohydrates: 27 gm., Fat: 1 gm., Percentage of calories from fat: 7%

Mushroom Boreck

Yields 12 to 16 triangles
PREP TIME: 1 hour
COOKING TIME: 25 to 30 minutes

Borecks are an Armenian turnover. Wild mushrooms add an exquisite flavor baked in this crisp, light pastry.

1 pound fresh button, shiitake, chanterelle,
   or oyster mushrooms, sliced (8 cups)

2 cloves garlic, minced

1 teaspoon olive oil .

1 bunch scallions, minced

3 cups cooked brown or basmati rice

1 pound soft tofu, mashed

½ teaspoon dried basil

1 teaspoon salt

pinch black pepper

½ bunch fresh parsley, minced

2 tablespoons fresh dill,
   or 1 teaspoon dried dill

2 carrots, grated

1 (1-pound) package filo dough

olive oil for brushing filo

1. Sauté mushrooms and garlic in olive oil until tender. Drain juices.

2. In a large mixing bowl combine cooked mushrooms and garlic with scallions, rice, tofu, basil, salt, pepper, parsley, dill, and carrots. Mix well.

3. To assemble Borecks, carefully unroll the stack of pastry sheets. Lay them flat on a work counter, and cover with plastic to prevent drying. Prepare a large clean surface next to the stack. Lay one sheet of pastry flat on the work surface. Use a soft pastry brush to lightly brush the sheet with olive oil. Use enough oil to barely moisten, but not saturate, the pastry sheets. Lay a second layer on top of the first, and again lightly brush with olive oil. Repeat with a third sheet. Cut through the three layers with a sharp knife lengthwise to produce two long strips.

4. Preheat oven to 350°F.

5. Spoon ½ cup filling onto lower right-hand corner of one of the strips. Fold that corner up toward left-hand edge to form a triangle, encasing the filling. Continue to roll up to the end of the strip until you have a triangular-shaped boreck. Brush the outside lightly with oil, and place on a cookie sheet. Continue to roll pastries until filling is used.

6. Bake 20 to 25 minutes until golden.

Per triangle: Calories: 190, Protein: 6 gm., Carbohydrates: 34 gm., Fat: 2 gm., Percentage of calories from fat: 9%

Mushroom Stroganoff

Serves 6 to 8
PREP TIME: 45 minutes
COOKING TIME: 20 minutes

This vegetarian version of a classic Russian dish is prepared without sour cream or meat. Serve over ribbon noodles, grains, or vegetables.

2 medium onions, finely chopped

1 tablespoon olive oil

½ pound button or shiitake mushrooms, sliced (4 cups)

2 cloves garlic, minced

¼ cup whole wheat flour

2 cups vegetable stock or water

2 tablespoons tamari

2 tablespoons tahini

1 tablespoon red miso

1 cup Tofu Sour Cream (pg 108)

½ teaspoon black pepper

½ teaspoon dill

½ teaspoon paprika

3 tablespoons fresh lemon juice

salt to taste

1. In a medium saucepan, sauté onions in olive oil until translucent. Add mushrooms and garlic, and sauté 3 minutes until mushrooms are tender. Sprinkle flour over vegetables and stir, coating mushrooms. Slowly add stock or water and tamari. Continue stirring. Bring to a boil, lower heat, and simmer 10 minutes.

2. Whisk in tahini, miso, Tofu Sour Cream, pepper, dill, paprika, and lemon juice. Heat slowly but do not boil. Serve immediately.

Per serving: Calories: 113 , Protein: 5 gm., Carbohydrates: 10 gm., Fat: 6 gm., Percentage of calories from fat: 48%

Pasta Fagioli

Serves 4 to 6
PREP TIME: 20 minutes
COOKING TIME: 2 hours

This classic pasta and bean dish is irresistible.

1 cup dried kidney, pinto, or anasazi beans
   (2 cups cooked beans)

6 cups water

1 teaspoon olive oil

1 onion, finely chopped

4 cloves garlic, minced

1 carrot, thinly sliced

1 green pepper, finely chopped

2 cups canned stewed tomatoes

1 teaspoon salt or to taste

1 pound pasta elbows, shells, or macaroni

3 tablespoons fresh basil, chopped

1. Soak beans overnight. Drain off soaking water, rinse beans, and drain again.

2. Put soaked beans into a large, heavy-bottomed soup pot with fresh water. Bring to a boil, lower heat, and simmer 1½ to 2 hours until beans are tender. Drain excess liquid, leaving enough to make a gravy-like consistency.

2. Sauté onions, garlic, carrots, and green pepper. Add vegetables, tomatoes, and salt to cooking beans, and simmer 20 minutes longer, stirring occasionally.

3. Cook pasta according to instructions on package.

4. Before serving, add fresh basil and pasta to beans. Stir gently and adjust seasonings.

Per serving: Calories: 246, Protein: 9 gm., Carbohydrates: 48 gm., Fat: 1 gm., Percentage of calories from fat: 4%

Polenta Torta

Serves 6 to 8
PREP TIME: 1½ hours
COOKING TIME: 1 hour

The elegant flavors of shiitake mushrooms, roasted red peppers, and sun-dried tomatoes create an impressive yet relatively simple entree for special guests.

1 recipe **Baked Polenta with Wild Mushrooms (pg 156), (follow recipe through step 3)**

1 recipe **Tofu Ricotta (pg 108)**

double recipe Sun-Dried Tomato and Basil Dressing (pg 103)

1 red bell pepper,
  or 1 (6 ounce) jar Italian roasted red peppers

6 ounces soy sausage, finely chopped (optional)

1 teaspoon olive oil

½ cup fresh basil, chopped

1. Prepare the Baked Polenta with Wild Mushroom recipe through step 3.

2. Preheat oven to 350°F.

3. Divide the polenta into two 9" x 12" oiled baking dishes. Spread polenta evenly in pans, and bake for 30 minutes. Remove polenta to cool for 20 minutes.

4. If you're roasting the pepper, turn the oven up to 400°F. Place the pepper on the cookie sheet, and roast for 45 minutes. Turn two or three times while roasting until evenly charred. Wrap charred pepper in a damp towel until cool enough to handle. Carefully peel away charred skin, and rinse well. Cut pepper lengthwise into thin strips.

5. In a small skillet, sauté soy sausage in oil until lightly browned. Stir in pepper strips and basil.

6. Preheat oven to 350°F.

7. To assemble Torta, spread one layer of baked polenta cake with half of the tomato dressing. Top with sausage mixture and spoon Tofu Ricotta over sausage layer. Using spatula to lift second polenta cake carefully out of baking dish, flip second polenta cake face down over tofu ricotta layer on the first polenta cake.

8. Drizzle half of the remaining dressing over top layer, cover with foil, and bake 30 minutes. Serve remaining dressing on the side.

Per serving: Calories: 316, Protein: 9 gm., Carbohydrates: 49 gm., Fat: 7 gm., Percentage of calories from fat: 20%

Pumpkin And Green Pea Curry

Serves 4 to 6
PREP TIME: 45 minutes
COOKING TIME: 45 minutes

This delicious, aromatic curry proves that pumpkins aren't just for pies. We recommend using organic pumpkins, available in the fall at vegetable and health food markets, or butternut squash when pumpkins are not available.

6 cups pumpkin or butternut squash, cubed

1 tablespoon canola oil

¾ cup onion, finely chopped

2 teaspoons whole brown mustard seeds

4 cloves garlic, minced

1 inch fresh gingerroot, minced

2 teaspoons ground cardamom

2 teaspoons garam masala (pg 15)

1 teaspoon ground fenugreek

1 teaspoon ground turmeric

1 teaspoon ground coriander

2 teaspoons salt

1 cup water

¼ cup fresh cilantro

1 cup frozen green peas, thawed

1. Peel, seed, scrape, and cube pumpkin or squash into 1-inch chunks.

2. Heat oil in a large, heavy saucepan. Sauté onion until soft.

3. Add mustard seeds and fry until seeds turn grey and pop. Add garlic, ginger, other spices, and salt. Sauté 2 minutes.

4. Add pumpkin and water. Cover and simmer 20 minutes until pumpkin is tender. Do not overcook.

5. Before serving, stir in green peas and fresh cilantro.

Per serving: Calories: 161, Protein: 4 gm., Carbohydrates: 29 gm., Fat: 3 gm., Percentage of calories from fat: 17%

Root Stew

Serves 6 to 8
PREP TIME: 45 minutes
COOKING TIME: 45 minutes

An easy, hearty, Oriental-flavored dish reminiscent of old-fashioned stews. Earthy root vegetables make a warming winter meal.

1 teaspoon sesame oil

8 cloves garlic, crushed

2 tablespoons fresh gingerroot, minced

3 large potatoes, cubed

3 carrots, cut in 1-inch chunks

2 yams or sweet potatoes, cubed

2 turnips, cubed

½ pound tofu, cubed

2 cups scallion bottoms, sliced (save greens for Oriental Slaw, pg 68)

1 bunch greens (turnip, collard, or kale), chopped

¼ cup tamari

1-2 tablespoons brown rice syrup or honey

2 tablespoons rice vinegar

2 tablespoons mirin or white wine (optional)

6-8 cups vegetable stock or water (depending on desired thickness of stew)

dash ground Szechuan or black pepper

1. Heat oil in a heavy pot. Sauté garlic and ginger until golden brown.

2. Stir in vegetables and add liquids.

3. Cover and simmer for 45 minutes over low flame until tender.

Per serving: Calories: 171, Protein: 4 gm., Carbohydrates: 34 gm., Fat: 1 gm., Percentage of calories from fat: 5%

Rigatoni
with Vegetable-Walnut Sauce

Serves 4 to 6
PREP TIME: 30 minutes
COOKING TIME: 20 minutes

1 clove garlic, minced

½ cup onion, thinly sliced

1 cup eggplant, cubed

1 tomato, chopped

1 cup broccoli florets

½ cup green pepper, thinly sliced

4 oyster mushrooms, quartered,
    or 2 ounces button mushrooms, sliced

1 teaspoon dried basil,
    or 1 tablespoon fresh basil, minced

1½ teaspoons salt to taste

pinch black pepper

1 tablespoon tamari

1 cup water

8 ounces uncooked rigatoni or ziti pasta

¼ cup walnuts, toasted

1. Combine all vegetables, basil, salt, pepper, and tamari with water in a large saucepan. Cover and simmer 15 minutes until tender.

2. Cook pasta according to instructions on package. Drain and spoon into a serving bowl or onto individual plates.

3. Spoon vegetables over pasta.

4. Garnish with toasted walnuts.

Per serving: Calories: 146, Protein: 5 gm., Carbohydrates: 21 gm., Fat: 2 gm., Percentage of calories from fat: 25%

Royal Tofu Roulade

Serves 6 to 8
PREP TIME: 1 hour (plus 2 hours in freezer)
COOKING TIME: 1 hour

Your friends and family will never miss the turkey at holiday time with this delectable, stuffed delight that takes tofu to new culinary heights.

2½ pounds firm tofu

½ cup tamari

egg replacer equivalent to 2 eggs (optional)

1 teaspoon curry powder

1 teaspoon rosemary

1 teaspoon sage

1 teaspoon thyme

1 teaspoon garlic powder

½ teaspoon salt

¼ teaspoon black pepper

dash Tabasco sauce

1 tablespoon olive oil or low-fat cooking spray

1 recipe Wild Rice Stuffing (pg 163)

1. Blend tofu with tamari, egg replacer, spices, salt, pepper, and Tabasco sauce in a food processor until smooth.

2. Cover a 9" x 14" cookie sheet with foil, and oil with olive oil or low-fat cooking spray.

3. Pour tofu mixture onto the cookie sheet, and spread evenly in a layer about ¼ inch thick. While spreading, press tofu into cookie sheet to smooth out any air pockets and creases. Cover with plastic wrap and place in freezer for 2 hours until completely frozen.

4. Preheat oven to 350°F.

5. Remove the plastic covering from tofu, and place the cookie sheet directly into oven. Bake 1 hour until a golden brown skin forms on the underside of the tofu.

6. Remove from oven and cool for 30 minutes.

7. After roulade has cooled, carefully turn whole tofu sheet onto a large piece of cheese cloth or thin towel so the underside of roulade is on top.

8. Using the cloth as a support to lift the roulade, slide a third of the longer end of the roulade onto a serving plate with the baked underside still facing up. The edge of tofu sheet should be covering three-quarters of the plate.

9. Hold the other two-thirds of the tofu sheet up, and have a helper spoon 6 cups of stuffing on top of roulade on the serving plate.

10. Form the stuffing into a cylinder that the remaining tofu sheet can easily roll around. Tuck the second side underneath, bringing long ends together. Gently pack in more stuffing from both ends. If the roulade begins to split, reposition it so the split area is underneath on the plate. If you need to trim the roulade, extra pieces can be served on the side or used for sandwiches.

11. Serve with Christmas Cranberry Glaze (page 77).

Per serving (using ½ recipe for stuffing): Calories: 258, Protein: 16 gm., Carbohydrates: 16 gm., Fat: 15 gm., Percentage of calories from fat: 49%

Sesame Soba Noodles

Serves 6
PREP TIME: 30 minutes
COOKING TIME: 6 to 8 minutes

This is a quick and easy "steam-fry" that's high in nutrition and flavor. Follow these basic directions, using any vegetables you have on hand.

12 cups water

1 pound buckwheat soba noodles

1 tablespoon sesame oil

1 small onion, thinly sliced in half moons

2 quarter-sized pieces of gingerroot, peeled and grated

4 tablespoons sesame seeds

½ cup carrots, julienned

½ cup red or green bell pepper, julienned

½ cup daikon or jicama, julienned (pgs 14-5)

2 tablespoons water

½ cup wild or domestic mushrooms, sliced

1 cup fresh spinach or chard, chopped

½ cup broccoli florets

2 tablespoons water

6 tablespoons tamari

¼ cup scallions, julienned

1. Bring 12 cups water to boil in a large pot. Add soba noodles and cook 4 to 6 minutes until al dente. Drain and rinse with cold water.

2. Heat sesame oil in a skillet. Add onions, ginger, and sesame seeds; sauté until onions are translucent and sesame seeds pop and turn golden. Add carrots, peppers, daikon or jicama, and water. Cover and steam 2 minutes. Add mushrooms, spinach or chard, broccoli, and another 2 tablespoons water, and steam 1 minute.

3. Add cooked soba noodles and tamari to vegetables. Stir and continue to steam-fry until noodles are hot. Top with scallions before serving.

Per serving: Calories: 168, Protein: 6 gm., Carbohydrates: 23 gm., Fat: 5 gm., Percentage of calories from fat: 27%

Spanokopita

Serves 6 to 8
PREP TIME: 1½ hours
COOKING TIME: 45 minutes

This dairy-free version of a Greek classic is a favorite at Shoshoni. Serve with Tabouli (pg 73) or Mudjedera (pg 151).

2 pounds fresh spinach

1 medium onion, minced

1 teaspoon olive oil

1 cup scallions, chopped

3 cups Tofu Feta (pg 107)

3 tablespoons fresh dill, chopped, or 2 teaspoons dried dill

½ cup fresh parsley, chopped

1 teaspoon salt

pinch black pepper

¼ teaspoon nutmeg

1 (1-pound package) filo dough

olive oil for brushing filo

1. Wash spinach well, remove stems, and steam in the water that clings to its leaves. Drain and squeeze out excess moisture. Chop finely and set aside.

2. Sauté onions in olive oil until translucent.

3. In a large mixing bowl, combine onions, scallions, Tofu Feta, dill, parsley, salt, pepper, and nutmeg. Mix in chopped spinach.

4. To assemble Spanokopitas, carefully unroll the filo. Lay the stack of pastry sheets flat on a work counter, and cover completely with plastic. Place a large cutting board or prepare a large clean surface next to the filo, and place a single layer of filo on the board. Lightly brush with olive oil. Place two more sheets on the first, brushing each lightly with oil, and covering the stack of filo each time a sheet is removed. Cut through the three layers with a sharp knife lengthwise to produce two long strips.

5. Preheat oven to 375°F.

6. Spoon ½ cup spinach filling onto lower right-hand corner of one of the strips. Fold corner toward left hand edge to form a triangle, encasing the filling. Continue to roll flag-style to the end of the strip until you have a triangular-shaped Spanikopita. Brush the outside lightly with oil, and place on a lightly oiled cookie sheet. Continue to roll pastries until filling is used.

7. Bake for 25 to 30 minutes until golden.

Per serving: Calories: 319, Protein: 14 gm., Carbohydrates: 49 gm., Fat: 7 gm., Percentage of calories from fat: 20%

Stuffed Swiss Chard

with Carrot Sauce

Serves 6 to 8
PREP TIME: 1 hour
COOKING TIME: 40 minutes

½ onion, finely chopped

3 cloves garlic, minced

2 cups mushrooms, sliced

½ cup water

7 medium potatoes, boiled, peeled, and mashed

1 bunch broccoli, chopped and steamed

1 green pepper, roasted or sautéed, and chopped

1 teaspoon salt

½ teaspoon black pepper

2 tablespoons fresh basil, chopped

6 large or 12 small leaves of Swiss chard, stems removed

½ cup water

1 recipe Carrot Sauce (pg 77)

1. Prepare potatoes, broccoli, and green peppers, and set aside.

2. Cook onion, garlic, and mushrooms in water until onions are translucent. Drain off liquid.

3. Mix mashed potatoes with onion mixture, steamed broccoli, and sautéed peppers. Add salt, pepper, and basil. Adjust seasonings to taste.

4. Preheat oven to 350°F.

5. If using large chard leaves, cut in half crosswise, making twelve 4-6 inch sections (leave small leaves whole). Stuff with potato mixture, rolling the filling inside like a crepe.

6. Place stuffed chard in a baking dish, add another ½ cup water, cover with foil, and bake for 40 to 50 minutes until heated throughout and chard is tender.

7. Warm Carrot Sauce in a small saucepan, and spoon over each chard roll.

Per serving: Calories: 199, Protein: 4 gm., Carbohydrates: 45 gm., Fat: 0 gm., Percentage of calories from fat: 0%

Sweet Corn And Coconut Curry

Serves 6 to 8
PREP TIME: 30 minutes
COOKING TIME: 1 hour

This intriguing curry uses the natural sweetness of corn, coconut, and roasted onion to balance the stronger masala curry spices.

1 onion, cut in half crosswise, outer skin removed

1 green pepper, cut in half lengthwise, seeds removed

½ cup tomatoes, chopped

2 teaspoons fresh gingerroot, grated

2 teaspoons ground cumin

½ teaspoon ground cardamom

2 teaspoons ground coriander

1 teaspoon turmeric

4 to 6 potatoes, boiled and cut into chunks

1 medium carrot, peeled and thinly sliced

3 cups fresh or frozen sweet corn kernels

2 ounces dried, unsweetened coconut, grated (⅔ cup)

½ cup soymilk

2 tablespoons honey

1½ teaspoons salt or to taste

1. Preheat oven to 375°F.

2. Roast onion and pepper by placing them cut side down on a cookie sheet and baking for 45 minutes.

3. Make a masala by blending roasted onion and green pepper with tomatoes and spices in a blender or food processor until smooth.

3. In a large saucepan, cook masala for 3 minutes. Add potatoes, carrot, corn, coconut, soymilk, and honey. Salt to taste and simmer 20 minutes. Stir occasionally and add a little water if needed.

Per serving: Calories: 254, Protein: 4 gm., Carbohydrates: 47 gm., Fat: 5 gm., Percentage of calories from fat: 18%

Tempeh Tandoori

Serves 3 to 4
PREP TIME: 20 minutes
COOKING TIME 30 - 45 minutes

This protein-rich, vegetarian curry is reminiscent of foods cooked in a North Indian Tandoori oven (an underground clay oven that gives foods a "smoked" flavor). Serve with basmati rice and vegetables.

1 pound tempeh, cut into rectangles,
   ½ "x 1" inch

1 cup onions, finely diced

1 teaspoon fresh garlic, minced

1 teaspoon canola oil

2 tablespoons curry powder

1 tablespoon ground cumin

½ cup tomato paste

2 tablespoons honey or brown rice syrup

2 teaspoons salt

¾ teaspoon cayenne

4 cups plain soy yogurt

½ cup frozen green peas, thawed

1. Sauté tempeh with ½ cup onion and garlic in canola oil until browned on the outside. Set aside.

2. Sauté ½ cup onion until translucent. Add curry powder and cumin, and cook 3 minutes. Whisk in tomato paste, honey, salt, and cayenne. Simmer 5 minutes, whisking occasionally.

3. Stir in soy yogurt and heat slowly on low. Add tempeh and peas, taking care not to overheat and curdle the yogurt.

Per serving: Calories: 407, Protein: 26 gm., Carbohydrates: 44 gm., Fat: 14 gm., Percentage of calories from fat: 31%

Vegetable-Tortilla Fold-Ups

Yields 12
PREP TIME: 1 hour
COOKING TIME: 30 minutes

A tasty lunch or dinner entree served with rice and beans or Mexican Corn Soup (page 54).

1 head cauliflower, cut in florets and steamed

6 red potatoes, boiled and mashed

2 onions, finely chopped

2 cloves garlic, minced

½ teaspoon cumin seeds

1 tablespoon olive oil

1½ cups raw washed greens (spinach, kale, chard, or collards)

1 green pepper, finely chopped

pinch red pepper seeds or cayenne

1 tablespoon ground cumin

2 teaspoons salt

½ teaspoon black pepper

1 tablespoon dried basil

12 large whole wheat tortillas

1. Prepare cauliflower and potatoes, and set aside.

2. Sauté onions, garlic, and cumin seeds in olive oil until onions are translucent. Add green pepper and sauté until tender. Add greens and cook until tender.

3. In a large mixing bowl, combine cooked cauliflower and potatoes with sautéed vegetables. Add red pepper seeds, cumin, salt, black pepper, and basil. Mix well and adjust seasonings to taste.

4. Lightly brush a skillet with oil, bring to medium heat, and warm each tortilla by briefly toasting on each side. As tortillas are warmed, stack and cover with a towel to keep warm and soft.

5. Spread ½ to ¾ cup filling on one half of tortilla and fold top over to form a half circle. Keep fold-ups warm in oven until serving. Serve with Pico de Gallo (page 93) or picante sauce.

Per fold-up: Calories: 166, Protein: 3 gm., Carbohydrates: 31 gm., Fat: 3 gm., Percentage of calories from fat: 16%

Tofu Lasagne

Serves 8 to 12
PREP TIME: 1½ hours
COOKING TIME: 45 minutes

Baked till bubbly, these tender layers of pasta, tofu, spinach, mushrooms, and tomato sauce with fresh herbs create a wonderful flavor. At Shoshoni we have a hard time convincing people there's no cheese in our recipe.

TOMATO SAUCE:

1 tablespoon olive oil

1 medium onion, finely chopped

2 cloves garlic, minced

1 medium eggplant, finely chopped

1 green bell pepper, finely chopped

24 ripe tomatoes, chopped,
   or 8 cups canned tomato puree

½ cup black olives, sliced

2 tablespoons tomato paste

1 teaspoon salt

½ teaspoon black pepper

1 tablespoon fresh oregano,
   or 1 teaspoon dried oregano

1 tablespoon fresh savory,
   or 1 teaspoon dried savory

1 tablespoon honey or brown rice syrup

1 tablespoon tamari

½ cup fresh basil, chopped

1. To prepare sauce, heat oil in a large saucepan. Sauté onion until translucent. Add garlic and eggplant, and sauté for 5 minutes until tender. Add peppers and sauté 3 minutes. Add tomatoes, olives, tomato paste, salt, black pepper, oregano, and savory. Bring to a boil, reduce heat, and simmer 20 to 30 minutes, stirring often until sauce thickens. Add honey, tamari, and fresh basil. Adjust seasonings to taste.

TOFU-SPINACH-MUSHROOM LAYER

2 pounds soft tofu

2 cups mushrooms, sliced

2 cloves garlic, minced

1 teaspoon salt

¼ teaspoon black pepper

½ teaspoon nutmeg

½ cup fresh basil, chopped

1 large bunch fresh spinach, washed, stems removed, blanched and chopped

1 pound lasagne noodles (semolina, whole wheat, or spinach)

2. To prepare tofu layer, blend tofu in food processor until smooth. In a saucepan, heat oil and sauté mushrooms, and garlic. Add tofu and simmer 3 minutes. Stir in salt, pepper, nutmeg, fresh basil, and cooked spinach. Adjust seasonings to taste.

3. Cook pasta according to instructions on box until al dente.

4. Preheat oven to 375°F.

5. To assemble lasagne, spread ¼ of the tomato sauce in a 13" x 9" x 2" baking pan. Place ¼ of the lasagne noodles over the sauce. Spread ⅓ of the tofu-spinach mixture over the pasta, then add another ¼ of the pasta. Repeat this process two more times, and end with a final layer of tomato sauce.

6. Bake lasagne for 45 minutes until hot throughout.

Per serving: Calories: 337, Protein: 16 gm., Carbohydrates: 47 gm., Fat: 9 gm., Percentage of calories from fat: 24%

Zucchini-Pine Nut Tamales

Yields 12 tamales
PREP TIME: 1½ hours
COOKING TIME: 1½ hours

Making tamales is a fun project to bring friends and family together. Worth the wait and the work, tamales are just the thing for special occasions and holidays. Serve the extra filling this makes as a warmed side dish or as a nice topping to the tamales themselves.

½ pound dried corn husks

1 medium onion, minced

5 cloves garlic, minced

½ cup green chilies, chopped

1 teaspoon olive oil

5 cups raw zucchini, grated

½ cup pine nuts, toasted

1 teaspoon salt

¼ teaspoon black pepper

½ pound Monterey Jack soy cheese, grated

3 tablespoons olive oil

2 cups masa harina

1 teaspoon salt

1½ teaspoons baking powder

1½ cups warm water or vegetable stock

1. Soak corn husks in hot water at least 1 hour, then drain and set aside. Shred 1 or 2 husks into 24 narrow strips, ¼ inch wide and 3 or more inches long. Natural fibers in the husks will guide the tears.

2. To prepare filling, sauté onions, garlic, and chilies in oil until onions are golden. Add squash and sauté until soft. Drain excess moisture by pressing mixture through a fine mesh colander, and cool. In a mixing bowl, combine squash mixture, pine nuts, salt, pepper, and soy cheese. Mix well and set aside.

3. To prepare dough, beat 3 tablespoons olive oil, masa harina, salt, and baking powder in a large bowl. Gradually add warm water or stock until dough forms a ball. The dough should have the consistency of moist pie dough.

4. Place water in bottom of a steamer, and bring to a boil while tamales are prepared. Keep water level below upper portion of steamer.

5. To prepare tamales, open a softened corn husk and spread 3 tablespoons masa harina dough in the center of the husk ¼ inch thick, leaving ½ inch of uncovered husk on the sides and 1 inch on the top and bottom. Place 1 tablespoon of filling in the

center of the dough. Wrap the dough and husk around the filling, and overlap sides of husk to seal. Tie both ends of husk with husk strips.

6. Place tamales vertically in the top part of the steamer (or horizontally if not stacked more than 2 deep), and cover.

7. Reduce flame to medium and steam 1 to 1½ hours. Add more water to the steamer as needed. The tamales are done when the husks fall cleanly away from the dough.

Per tamale: Calories: 223, Protein: 6 gm., Carbohydrates: 24 gm., Fat: 11 gm., Percentage of calories from fat: 44%

Tofu In A Pocket

Serves 4
PREP TIME: 20 minutes
COOKING TIME: 10 minutes

Whole wheat pitas stuffed with cheesy Scrambled Tofu make a hearty brunch. Or serve with a steamy bowl of soup for a satisfying lunch.

1 recipe Scrambled Tofu (pg 28)

4 ounces cheddar soy cheese, grated

4 whole wheat pitas

8 slices tomato

8 small lettuce leaves

4 tablespoons soy mayonnaise

1. Prepare Scrambled Tofu, adding soy cheese at the end of cooking time. Cover and set aside.

2. Preheat oven to 225°F.

3. Heat pitas in the oven for a few minutes until warmed through but not crisp. Cut breads in half and spread the inside of each pocket with soy mayonnaise. Fill each pocket with scrambled tofu, lettuce leaves, and tomato slices.

Per serving: Calories: 482, Protein: 21 gm., Carbohydrates: 37 gm., Fat: 27 gm., Percentage of calories from fat: 50%

SIDE DISHES

Guests at Shoshoni often remark on the variety of foods served at each meal. The side dishes in this section each have their own character. Serve them with an entree, or put them together into interesting combinations. It's a new way to look at meals. Select a bean, a grain, and a vegetable dish that sound good to you and go well together to compose your own nutritious vegan meal. For example, a popular selection we would serve at Shoshoni would include Baked Polenta with Wild Mushrooms, Anasazi Beans, and Cauliflower and Peas.

African Red Beans

Yields 8 cups
PREP TIME: 30 minutes
COOKING TIME: 2 hours

These beans are extraordinary. We use homemade almond milk to create the nutty, rich flavor of this traditional dish. Serve with rice, couscous, or flat bread.

2 cups red beans, dried (4 cups cooked)

6 cups water

2 tomatoes, cut in wedges

1 teaspoon olive oil

2 onions, finely chopped

½ cup celery, finely chopped

1 medium potato, peeled and cubed

1 cup almonds

1½ cups soymilk

1 teaspoon salt

½ teaspoon cayenne or to taste

black pepper to taste

1. Soak beans overnight in cool water. Drain and put into a large, heavy-bottomed soup pot with water and tomatoes. Bring to a boil, lower heat, and simmer 1 ½ to 2 hours until tender. Add more water if needed, using just enough to keep beans covered, but cooking off enough so liquid is reduced to a gravy-like consistency at the end of cooking time.

2. Sauté onions, celery, and potatoes in olive oil for 15 minutes until potatoes are almost soft. Set aside.

3. Puree almonds and soymilk in a blender until smooth.

4. Add sautéed vegetables, almond milk, salt, cayenne, and black pepper to cooked beans, and simmer 20 to 30 minutes.

Per cup: Calories: 280, Protein: 11 gm., Carbohydrates: 34 gm., Fat: 11 gm., Percentage of calories from fat: 35%

Anasazi Beans

Serves 6 to 8
PREP TIME: 20 minutes
COOKING TIME: 2 hours

These colorful beans are named after the Anasazi Indians. Anasazi means "ancient ones," and we can only speculate that these were a staple food of this ancient Pueblo culture. The beans are deep burgundy with bright white flecks like a pinto bean. They are very tender with a delicious flavor that needs little seasoning.

2 cups dried anasazi beans (4 cups cooked)

8 cups water

1 medium onion, minced

3 cloves garlic, minced

1 Anaheim chili pepper, minced

1 teaspoon olive oil

1 teaspoon salt

pinch black pepper

1. Rinse beans well and soak overnight in enough cold water to cover.

2. Drain beans and put into a large, heavy-bottomed soup pot with 8 cups fresh water. Bring to a boil, lower heat, and simmer for 1 ½ hours until beans are tender.

3. Sauté onion, garlic, and chili in oil. Add to beans and simmer for 30 more minutes. There should be enough liquid to make a gravy-like consistency.

4. Before serving, add chopped fresh cilantro or top with Pico de Gallo (page 93).

5. To make refried beans, drain liquid after cooking and mash beans, adding cumin and chili powder to taste.

Per serving: Calories: 147, Protein: 7 gm., Carbohydrates: 27 gm., Fat: 1 gm., Percentage of calories from fat: 6%

Black-Eyed Peas And Greens

Serves 6
PREP TIME: 20 minutes
COOKING TIME: 2 hours

We adapted a simple version of this down-home favorite that pleases our Southern visitors. This dish is at its traditional best served with Crispy Southern Corn Bread (page 177) and baked yams.

3 cups black-eyed peas, dried

8 cups water

2 bay leaves

2 small onions, thinly sliced

3 cloves garlic, minced

1 teaspoon olive oil

2 teaspoons sage

2 teaspoons thyme

6 packed cups kale, collard, or mustard greens, chopped

2 teaspoon salt

pinch black pepper

4 dashes Tabasco sauce

1 tablespoon apple cider or raspberry vinegar

1. Soak peas overnight in cool water; drain and rinse well. In a large, heavy-bottomed pot, bring water, bay leaves, and peas to a boil. Lower heat and simmer for 1 hour. Add more water as needed.

2. Sauté onions and garlic in olive oil until translucent. Add sautéed onions, sage, and thyme to peas and simmer 30 minutes.

3. Add greens, salt, pepper, and Tabasco sauce, and simmer 30 minutes longer. There should be enough liquid to keep peas moist but not soupy. Add vinegar before serving.

Per serving: Calories: 290, Protein: 15 gm., Carbohydrates: 52 gm., Fat: 2 gm., Percentage of calories from fat: 6%

Lentil Sambar

Serves 6 to 8
PREP TIME: 30 minutes
COOKING TIME: 1 hour

Sambar, a thick, curried lentil and vegetable soup, can be served with homemade chapatis or basmati rice.

6 cups water

1 cup dried lentils

1 cup onions, minced

1 cup carrot, thinly sliced

1 cup cauliflower florets

1 tomato, diced

2 teaspoons salt

½ teaspoon ground cumin

½ teaspoon ground coriander

½ teaspoon turmeric

pinch cayenne

1 tablespoon canola oil

2 tablespoons shredded coconut, fresh or
    dried

1 tablespoon whole black or
    brown mustard seeds

1 tablespoon whole cumin seeds

⅛ teaspoon asafetida

2 tablespoons lemon juice

1. Bring water to boil in a large, heavy-bottomed pot. Rinse lentils and add to water. Bring to a boil, reduce heat, and simmer 30 minutes.

2. Add vegetables, salt, ground cumin, coriander, turmeric, and cayenne.

3. In a small skillet, heat oil and fry coconut and mustard seeds until seeds turn grey and start to pop. Add cumin seeds and fry until golden. Add asafetida and remove from heat. Stir spice mixture into lentils, and simmer on low 30 minutes.

4. Before serving, stir in lemon juice and adjust seasonings.

Per serving: Calories: 158, Protein: 7 gm., Carbohydrates: 21 gm., Fat: 4 gm., Percentage of calories from fat: 23%

Mudjedera

Serves 4 to 6
PREP TIME: 20 minutes
COOKING TIME: 1 hour

This Armenian lentil and bulghur wheat pilaf provides a rich protein combination. Serve with Moroccan Vegetable Tagine (page 126) or Aegean Vegetables (page 164). Mudjedera also makes a delicious cold salad with the addition of fresh lemon juice, tomatoes, cucumber slices, and crumbled Tofu Feta (page 107).

½ cup dried lentils

1¾ cups vegetable stock or water

¼ cup fine bulghur

1 onion, thinly sliced

1 teaspoon olive oil

pinch cayenne

salt and pepper to taste

1. Cover lentils with water and soak 5 minutes. Discard beans that float and drain off soaking water.

2. In a heavy-bottomed pot, bring lentils to a boil in stock. Lower heat and simmer until tender (45 minutes to 1 hour). Stir in bulghur and add water to barely cover. Cook over low heat 5 minutes, remove from heat, cover, and let stand 10 minutes.

3. Sauté onions in olive oil until tender. Stir half the sautéed onions into pilaf, and season with cayenne, salt, and pepper. Garnish pilaf with remaining sautéed onions.

Per serving: Calories: 119, Protein: 6 gm., Carbohydrates: 21 gm., Fat: 1 gm., Percentage of calories from fat: 8%

Pinto Beans

Yields 8 cups
PREP TIME: 20 minutes
COOKING TIME: 2 hours

This bean dish can be served as is with rice or mashed into refried beans for making burritos, tacos, and tostadas.

2 cups dried pinto beans, (4 cups cooked)

8 cups water

2 onions, finely chopped

3 cloves garlic, minced

2 carrots, thinly sliced

1 green pepper, finely chopped

½ jalapeño pepper, minced

2 teaspoons olive oil

1½ teaspoons salt or to taste

2 teaspoons ground cumin

2 teaspoons basil

⅓ cup fresh cilantro, chopped

1. Soak beans overnight in enough water to cover. Drain and rinse beans and put into a large, heavy-bottomed soup pot with fresh water. Bring to a boil, lower heat, and simmer for 1½ to 2 hours until tender.

2. Sauté onions, garlic, carrots, green pepper, and jalapeño in olive oil. Add vegetables, salt, cumin, and basil to beans, and simmer 30 minutes longer, stirring occasionally. There should be enough liquid in beans to make a gravy-like consistency.

3. Before serving, adjust seasonings to taste, and stir in fresh cilantro.

4. To make refried beans, drain liquid after cooking, and mash beans or blend in a food processor to desired consistency.

Per cup: Calories: 179, Protein: 8 gm., Carbohydrates: 33 gm., Fat: 1 gm., Percentage of calories from fat: 5%

Savory Lentils

Serves 6 to 8
PREP TIME: 20 minutes
COOKING TIME: 1 hour

Enjoy the simplicity of lentils in this mildly flavored dal.

2 cups dried lentils

6 cups water

½ cup rolled oats

1 medium onion, minced

1 tablespoon canola oil

5 cloves garlic, minced

1 tablespoon cumin seeds

1½ teaspoons caraway seeds

1 tablespoon curry powder

1 carrot, peeled and thinly sliced

¼ cup fresh parsley, minced

2 tablespoons fresh lemon juice

1 cup soy yogurt (optional)

1. Soak lentils overnight in enough cold water to cover. Drain and rinse well.

2. Bring 6 cups water to a boil. Add lentils and oats, and bring to a boil again. Lower heat and simmer 30 minutes.

3. In a small skillet, sauté onion in canola oil until translucent. Add garlic, cumin seeds, and caraway seeds, and sauté until golden. Add the onion mixture, curry powder, carrots, and parsley to lentils. Simmer 20 to 30 minutes.

4. Before serving, stir in lemon juice and soy yogurt, if desired.

Per serving: Calories: 231, Protein: 13 gm., Carbohydrates: 37 gm., Fat: 3 gm., Percentage of calories from fat: 12%

Shoshoni Red Lentil Dal

Serves 4 to 6
PREP TIME: 30 minutes
COOKING TIME: 30 minutes

Dal and rice is the staple food of India, providing a high protein meal in a largely vegetarian culture. Traveling in India, we found the varieties and flavors of the dals exciting and satisfying. In the States, it is still our favorite meal.

1 cup dried red lentils

4 cups water

¾ inch fresh gingeroot, thinly grated

1 teaspoon canola oil

2 teaspoons cumin seeds

½ teaspoon fennel seeds (optional)

2 teaspoons whole brown mustard seeds

2 cloves garlic, minced

1 teaspoon curry powder

½ teaspoon cardamom, ground

½ teaspoon coriander, ground

pinch cinnamon

pinch clove

½ teaspoon salt

2 medium tomatoes, finely chopped

1 tablespoon fresh lemon juice

¼ cup fresh cilantro, chopped (optional)

1. In a fine mesh colander, rinse lentils well. Place lentils and water in a pot, and cook for 20 minutes until lentils soften.

2. Heat oil until very hot but not smoking. Drop in seeds. Cover and remove from heat. Shake pan until popping stops. Uncover, stir in garlic, and cook until golden. Stir in spices, ginger, salt, and tomatoes.

3. Stir spice mixture into cooked lentils, and continue to cook on low heat for ten minutes.

4. Before serving, add fresh lemon juice and cilantro, if desired. Serve with basmati rice and chapatis.

Per serving: Calories: 156, Protein: 10 gm., Carbohydrates: 26 gm., Fat: 1 gm., Percentage of calories from fat: 6%

Split Pea Dal

Serves 6 to 8
PREP TIME: 20 minutes
COOKING TIME: 2 hours

This popular dish from North India is a staple in the diet of many monasteries when served with rice and potato curry.

1½ cups dried yellow split peas

5 cups water

1 tablespoon sesame or canola oil

1 tablespoon black mustard seeds

1 tablespoon cumin seeds

1 clove garlic, minced

¼ teaspoon turmeric

¼ teaspoon chili paste (or pinch of cayenne)

½ teaspoon ground cumin

½ teaspoon ground coriander

1 tomato, finely chopped

1 teaspoon salt or to taste

1 cup soy yogurt (optional)

1. Rinse split peas. Bring water to boil in a large pot, and add peas. Return to boil, stir, then lower heat, and simmer 1½ to 2 hours until tender.

2. In a skillet, heat oil and sauté mustard seeds until they "pop" and turn grey. Add cumin seeds and fry until golden. Add garlic, turmeric, chili paste or cayenne, ground cumin, and coriander. Sauté 2 minutes.

3. Add spices, salt, and tomato to peas, and cook 30 minutes.

4. Before serving, stir in soy yogurt, if desired.

Per serving: Calories: 165, Protein: 9 gm., Carbohydrates: 25 gm., Fat: 2 gm., Percentage of calories from fat: 11%

Baked Polenta
with Wild Mushrooms

Serves 6
PREP TIME: 20 minutes
COOKING TIME: 1 hour

This hearty, baked grain dish originally comes from the northern Italian countryside. If you are unable to find polenta (a coarsely ground cornmeal) at your grocery store, regular cornmeal may be substituted.

5 cups water

2 cups uncooked polenta or cornmeal

1 tablespoon salt

6 cloves garlic, minced

1 large onion, finely chopped

1 teaspoon olive oil

4 cups wild mushrooms, chopped (porcini, morels, etc.)*

pinch black pepper

⅓ cup fresh basil

Shiitake or button mushrooms may be substituted for wild varieties.

1. In a saucepan or kettle, bring 5 cups of water to a boil. In a separate, heavy-bottomed saucepan, mix 3 cups of the boiling water with polenta and salt, and heat over medium-low flame. When well mixed, whisk in remaining 2 cups boiling water. Continue whisking 5 minutes until smooth and thick. If polenta is still hard and grainy, continue cooking over low heat. Add more water if necessary.

2. In a small skillet, sauté garlic and onion in oil until translucent. Add mushrooms and sauté. Stir in pepper and basil.

3. Preheat oven to 350°F.

4. Stir mushroom mixture into polenta.

5. Turn into an oiled 9" x 12" baking dish. Bake 15 to 25 minutes or until a golden crust forms.

Per serving: Calories: 196, Protein: 5 gm., Carbohydrates: 40 gm., Fat: 1 gm., Percentage of calories from fat: 5%

Brown Rice Crepes

Serves 4 to 6
PREP TIME: 10 minutes
COOKING TIME: 15 to 20 minutes

Most often used for Masala Dosa (page 124), these crepes can also accompany vegetable curries and stews.

2 cups cooked brown rice

1½ cups water

¼ teaspoon salt

**¼ cup brown rice flour or
whole wheat flour**

1. Puree rice, water, salt, and flour in a blender until smooth.

2. Let mixture stand 30 minutes.

3. Heat a griddle or cast iron skillet, coat lightly with oil, and ladle ¼ cup of the batter onto the skillet. Brown on both sides.

Per serving: Calories: 112, Protein: 3 gm., Carbohydrates: 24 gm., Fat: 0 gm., Percentage of calories from fat: 0%

Festival Rice

Serves 4 to 6
PREP TIME: 25 minutes
COOKING TIME: 25 minutes

Don't wait for a special occasion to serve this colorful, aromatic rice pilaf. It's simple to prepare and perfect served with assorted curries.

2 cups water

1 cup uncooked basmati rice

1 tablespoon canola oil

2 tablespoons sesame seeds

4 tablespoons slivered almonds

½ cup shredded coconut, cooked or dried

6 whole cloves

1 cinnamon stick or ¼ teaspoon ground cinnamon

4 cardamom pods

1 cup carrots, grated

1 teaspoon salt

3 tablespoons raisins or currants

½ cup frozen green peas, thawed

1. Rinse rice and set aside. Heat water in a large, heavy-bottomed pot with a tight-fitting lid.

2. In a small skillet, heat oil and fry sesame seeds, almonds, coconut, cloves, cinnamon, and cardamom until coconut turns light brown. Add rice and cook a few minutes longer, stirring constantly.

3. Bring water to a boil. Add rice mixture, carrots, salt, and raisins. Return to a boil, stir, then reduce heat to low. Cover tightly, and cook 20 to 25 minutes.

4. Allow rice to sit 10 minutes, then remove whole spices that have surfaced to the top. Stir in green peas before serving.

Per serving: Calories: 397, Protein: 7 gm., Carbohydrates: 41 gm., Fat: 23 gm., Percentage of calories from fat: 52%

Golden Saffron Rice

Serves 4 to 6
PREP TIME: 15 minutes
COOKING TIME: 30 minutes

Fragrant basmati rice with aromatic spices creates an exotic, easy-to-prepare dish. A regal accompaniment to simple vegetables or a perfect mate to Indian curries.

2 cups water

¼ teaspoon freshly grated gingerroot or powdered ginger

¼ teaspoon saffron threads

¼ teaspoon ground turmeric

¼ teaspoon ground cardamom

¼ teaspoon powdered garlic

¼ teaspoon ground cumin

¼ teaspoon ground coriander

**1 cup uncooked basmati rice
   (2 cups cooked rice)**

½ cup frozen green peas, thawed

1. Bring 2 cups water to a boil, and add saffron and spices.

2. Put basmati rice into fine mesh strainer, and rinse well with cool water.

3. Add rice to boiling, spiced water. Stir well and reduce heat to low. Cover and simmer for 20 minutes.

4. Allow rice to sit for another 5 minutes, then stir in green peas before serving.

Per serving: Calories: 105, Protein: 3 gm., Carbohydrates: 23 gm., Fat: 0 gm., Percentage of calories from fat: 0%

Kasha With Raisins And Walnuts

Yields 8 cups
PREP TIME: 20 minutes
COOKING TIME: 30 minutes

Kasha is another name for roasted buckwheat groats. This hearty side dish is delicious served with a medley of vegetables.

1 tablespoon olive oil

1 cup kasha

½ cup water

1 onion, thinly sliced in half moons

½ cup raisins

2 cups water

½ cup walnuts, toasted

½ teaspoon salt

¼ teaspoon black pepper

2 teaspoons basil

2 tablespoons tamari

1. Heat oil in a heavy-bottomed pot, and sauté kasha, stirring frequently, until browned.

2. In a separate pot, steam onions and raisins in ½ cup water until tender, and set aside.

3. Bring 2 cups water to a boil, and slowly add to kasha. Cover, turn heat to low, and simmer 20 minutes. Stir in steamed onions and raisins, toasted walnuts, salt, pepper, basil, and tamari. Continue cooking, uncovered, for 10 minutes.

Per cup: Calories: 122, Protein: 2 gm., Carbohydrates: 14 gm., Fat: 6 gm., Percentage of calories from fat: 44%

Ole! Pozole

Serves 4 to 6
PREP TIME: 45 minutes
COOKING TIME: 1 to 4 hours

Pozole is a type of white corn also known as hominy. Dried pozole looks like huge kernels of corn. This side dish, popular in Mexico and the Southwest, is traditionally made with pork and served on Christmas Eve. Our delicious vegetarian version uses tofu sausage.

1 cup dried pozole

8 cups water

2 dried whole ancho chilies (sun-dried red chilies)

1 teaspoon olive oil

1 medium onion, thinly sliced

4 cloves fresh garlic, minced

1 tablespoon whole cumin seed

4 tomatillos (Mexican green tomatoes), peeled and chopped

8 links of tofu sausage, sliced in ¼ inch rounds

1 tablespoon dried sage

1 teaspoon salt

¼ teaspoon black pepper

¼ cup fresh cilantro, chopped

1. Soak pozole overnight in enough cool water to cover. Drain soaking liquid. In a heavy-bottomed pot, combine pozole with 8 cups fresh water, and cook for 3 hours. Add ancho chilies to cooking pozole; chilies will simply dissolve. Taste cooking water after 1 hour. If mixture is getting too hot, remove the chilies.

2. Heat oil in a skillet and sauté onions, garlic, and cumin seed until golden. Add tomatillos and cook until they soften and blend with onion. Add tofu sausage and cook until browned.

3. When pozole is tender, add vegetable mixture and all remaining spices except fresh cilantro. Simmer on low for 30 to 45 minutes.

4. Garnish with fresh cilantro before serving.

QUICK VERSION

Substitute 4 cups of canned hominy for dried pozole. Substitute ½ cup canned Mexican green tomatoes for tomatillos. Substitute 1 teaspoon chili powder and ¼ teaspoon cayenne for the ancho chilies. Follow above directions and cut out initial pozole cooking time.

Per serving: Calories: 188, Protein: 8 gm., Carbohydrates: 16 gm., Fat: 10 gm., Percentage of calories from fat: 48%

Whole Wheat Noodles
with Sesame and Garlic

Serves 3 to 4
PREP TIME: 30 minutes
COOKING TIME: 6 to 8 minutes

A quick and easy pasta side dish.

12 ounces whole wheat noodles

2 tablespoons sesame oil

½ cup sesame seeds

6 cloves garlic, minced

6 quarts salted water

1. Bring water to a rapid boil. Add noodles and bring to a boil once again. Stir and cook 5 to 8 minutes or until al dente. Drain pasta in a colander, and rinse with cool water.

2. Heat sesame oil in a large skillet. Add sesame seeds and cook until golden brown. Add garlic and sauté until barely brown.

3. Toss pasta into pan with sesame seeds, and stir rapidly with a wooden spoon to coat noodles with garlic and seeds. Serve immediately.

Per serving: Calories: 330, Protein: 9 gm., Carbohydrates: 33 gm., Fat: 17 gm., Percentage of calories from fat: 46%

Wild Rice Stuffing

Yields 6 to 8 servings for Royal Tofu Roulade (page 134), with extra as a side dish.
PREP TIME: 30 minutes
COOKING TIME: 1 hour

The soy sausage flavor brings out the best in this savory stuffing, adding a traditional touch to your holiday feast.

8 cups water

1 pound (4 cups) uncooked wild rice

1½ ounces dried shiitake mushrooms

2 cups water

1 cup onions, minced

8 cloves fresh garlic, minced

1 (10-oz.) package soy sausage, sliced

2 tablespoons canola oil

1 tablespoon dried rosemary

1 tablespoon dried thyme,
  or ¼ cup fresh thyme, chopped

1 tablespoon dried sage,
  or ¼ cup fresh sage, chopped

1 tablespoon dried winter savory,
  or ¼ cup fresh savory, chopped

1 tablespoon salt

1 teaspoon celery seed

½ teaspoon black pepper

¼ cup fresh parsley, minced

2 ounces dried organic cherries (optional)

1 cup herb stuffing mix or leftover
  corn bread

1. Bring water to a boil in a 4-quart saucepan. Add wild rice and return to a boil, then lower heat and simmer rice for 40 minutes. The rice is done when it's soft and the liquid has been absorbed. Drain excess water and set aside.

2. Soak mushrooms in 2 cups of warm water for 20 minutes. When soft, drain and save liquid, being careful not to pour off any grit or sand from soaking. Slice mushrooms thinly.

3. In a large, heavy pot, sauté onions, garlic, soy sausage, and mushrooms in oil until onions are translucent. Add spices and herbs.

4. Add mushroom liquid and cherries, then bring to a boil.

5. Add stuffing mix and rice. Stir well. Simmer for 3 to 4 minutes until liquid is absorbed.

Per serving: Calories: 235, Protein: 9 gm., Carbohydrates: 18 gm., Fat: 13 gm., Percentage of calories from fat: 50%

Aegean Vegetables

Serves 6 to 8
PREP TIME: 30 minutes
COOKING TIME: 30 minutes

This colorful dish is delightful served with wedges of pita bread, Mudjedera (page 151), or couscous.

2 garlic cloves, minced

2 small onions, thinly sliced

1 teaspoon olive oil

1 eggplant, peeled and cut in 1-inch cubes

1 green pepper, thinly sliced

2 large ripe tomatoes, cut in 8 wedges each

2 stalks celery, sliced

**2 teaspoons fresh basil,
    or ½ teaspoon dried basil**

¼ teaspoon cinnamon

¼ teaspoon coriander

1 teaspoon fresh parsley, minced

1 teaspoon fresh lemon juice

salt and pepper to taste

1. Sauté garlic and onions in olive oil until translucent.

2. Add eggplant and sauté until tender.

3. Add green pepper, tomatoes, celery, basil, cinnamon, coriander, parsley, lemon juice, and salt and pepper. Cook slowly 10 minutes or until vegetables are tender. Do not overcook.

4. Let stand 10 minutes to allow flavors to blend.

Per serving: Calories: 46, Protein: 1 gm., Carbohydrates: 9 gm., Fat: 0 gm., Percentage of calories from fat: 0%

Cauliflower And Peas
with Soy Yogurt

Serves 6
PREP TIME: 15 minutes
COOKING TIME: 10 minutes

This mildly seasoned, versatile side dish goes especially well with spicy entrees.

1 head cauliflower, cut in florets

1 cup frozen green peas, thawed

½ cup soy yogurt

½ teaspoon sage

½ teaspoon salt

pinch black pepper

pinch cinnamon

1. Steam cauliflower 5 to 8 minutes until tender.

2. Add peas, soy yogurt, and spices. Cook over low 2 to 3 minutes until yogurt is warm. Do not boil or yogurt will curdle.

3. Serve warm.

Per serving: Calories: 45, Protein: 2 gm., Carbohydrates: 8 gm., Fat: 0 gm., Percentage of calories from fat: 0%

Green Beans With Cashews

Serves 4 to 6
PREP TIME: 15 minutes
COOKING TIME: 25 minutes

Fresh green beans tossed with crunchy cashews make a tasty accompaniment to any entree.

4 cups fresh green beans, cut in
    2-inch long pieces

½ cup onion, thinly sliced

1 clove garlic, minced

1 carrot, thinly sliced

½ cup cashews, toasted

2 tablespoons fresh cilantro, minced

juice of one orange

½ teaspoon salt

pinch black pepper

½ teaspoon ground coriander

1. Steam green beans, onion, garlic, and carrots 15 to 20 minutes until beans are tender.

2. Add cashews, cilantro, orange juice, salt, pepper, and coriander to beans. Stir well and simmer 5 minutes.

Per serving: Calories: 131 , Protein: 4 gm., Carbohydrates: 15 gm., Fat: 6 gm., Percentage of calories from fat: 41%

Miniature Harvest Pumpkins

Filled with Creamed Swiss Chard

Serves 6 to 8
PREP TIME: 1 hour
COOKING TIME: 1 hour

Serve these wonderful baby pumpkins with a holiday feast or as a main course. Fill them with dairy-free creamed chard, a cool season vegetable rich in vitamins and calcium.

8 baby pumpkins

6 quarts water

3 pounds fresh Swiss chard or spinach

4 shallots or 1 small onion

2 tablespoons olive oil

4 tablespoons pastry flour

2 cups hot water

½ teaspoon sea salt

1 tablespoon light miso

⅛ teaspoon black pepper

⅛ teaspoon nutmeg

1. Wash and dry baby pumpkins.

2. In a large pot, bring water to a boil. Add the pumpkins and boil gently for 20 minutes. Remove the pumpkins with a slotted spoon or tongs, and allow them to cool.

3. Carve a circle around the stem, remove the "lid" like a Halloween pumpkin, and set aside. With a teaspoon remove seeds and inner stringy pulp.

4. Place hollow pumpkins in a glass casserole pan, and set aside until ready to fill.

5. Wash chard well and remove thick stems. Place wet chard in a large pot, and steam in the water that clings to the leaves for 5 minutes. Drain cooked chard and press or squeeze out any excess moisture. When greens have cooled, chop them finely.

6. Peel and mince shallots or onions. In a heavy saucepan, heat oil and sauté shallots over medium heat until transparent.

7. Add flour and stir with a wire whisk, allowing flour to toast lightly. Slowly add 2 cups hot water, and continue to whisk vigorously to smooth out lumps.

8. Bring to a boil, then lower heat, and add seasonings. Continue to simmer for 3 to 4 minutes until sauce thickens. Stir in cooked chard and simmer for another 5 minutes.

9. Before serving, heat pumpkins in the oven at 350°F, and place on a serving dish. Fill each pumpkin with several spoonfuls of creamed chard.

Per serving: Calories: 133, Protein: 5 gm., Carbohydrates: 17 gm., Fat: 4 gm., Percentage of calories from fat: 27%

Parsleyed Potatoes

Serves 4 to 6
PREP TIME: 15 minutes
COOKING TIME: 30 to 45 minutes

These potatoes get their creamy texture from soymilk. Use baby new potatoes when available.

**10-12 small new potatoes,
   or 4-6 medium potatoes**

1 cup plain soymilk

4 tablespoons fresh parsley, minced

3 scallions, minced

salt and pepper to taste

1. Boil potatoes until soft. Cut new potatoes in half and larger potatoes into chunks.

2. In a medium saucepan, combine potatoes with soymilk, parsley, scallions, salt, and pepper. Heat slowly and serve.

Per serving: Calories: 156 , Protein: 3 gm., Carbohydrates: 34 gm., Fat: 1 gm., Percentage of calories from fat: 6%

BAKERY

The art of bread baking is ancient and varied. Many of the long-time yogis at our Ashrams, including Swami Shambhavananda, began their spiritual practice as bakers. Somehow the two go hand-in-hand. Consequently, the aroma of freshly baked bread fills the lodge from morning to night. Shoshoni breads vary from complex, yeasted varieties to super-easy quick breads, muffins, and cookies prepared without eggs or dairy products. We chose a few simple breads and specialty breads for you to try.

Tips For Baking Bread:

Use the flours specified in the recipes.

Use the specified amount of yeast.

Water temperature should range between 105°F and 115°F.

Have dry ingredients at room temperature.

Knead the dough thoroughly.

Before baking, allow the bread to rise completely, doubling in size.

Cover the rising dough to prevent it from drying out.

Bake bread in a preheated oven at moderate to high temperature.

For high altitude baking, more flour may be used.

Aloha Muffins

Yields 12 muffins
PREP TIME: 25 minutes
COOKING TIME: 30 minutes

Dream of the Islands when you eat these muffins.

½ cup soft tofu

2 large, ripe bananas

⅔ cup pineapple juice concentrate

egg replacer equivalent to 1 egg (optional)

2 cups whole wheat pastry flour

2 teaspoons baking powder

½ teaspoon baking soda

1 teaspoon cinnamon

¼ teaspoon nutmeg

¼ teaspoon salt

¾ cup Macadamia nuts or walnuts,
   chopped

½ cup fresh or dried papaya,
   diced (optional)

1 cup fresh or canned pineapple, crushed

1. Preheat oven to 375°F.

2. Blend tofu, bananas, juice, and egg replacer in food processor.

3. Combine flour, baking powder, baking soda, cinnamon, nutmeg, and salt in large bowl.

4. Stir tofu mixture into flour mixture, and blend well with large wooden spoon. Fold in nuts and fruits.

5. Spoon batter into oiled muffin tins, and bake 25 to 30 minutes.

6. Cool 10 minutes before removing from tins.

Per muffin: Calories: 155, Protein: 5 gm., Carbohydrates: 22 gm., Fat: 5 gm., Percentage of calories from fat: 29%

Blueberry Oatmeal Muffins

Yields 12 muffins
PREP TIME: 15 minutes
COOKING TIME: 30 minutes

These light and delicious muffins make a nutritious breakfast or afternoon snack.

½ cup soft tofu

2 large ripe bananas

⅔ cup apple juice concentrate

egg replacer equivalent to 1 egg (optional)

1 teaspoon vanilla extract

¾ cup whole wheat flour

¾ cup oat flour

½ cup oat bran

¼ cup rolled oats

2 teaspoons baking powder

½ teaspoon baking soda

1 teaspoon cinnamon

¼ teaspoon salt

2 cups fresh or frozen blueberries

1. Preheat oven to 375°F.

2. Cream tofu, bananas, juice, egg replacer, and vanilla in food processor or mixer.

3. Combine flours, bran, oats, baking powder, baking soda, cinnamon, and salt in a large bowl.

4. Stir tofu mixture into flour mixture, and blend well with large wooden spoon. Fold in blueberries.

5. Spoon batter into oiled muffin tins, and bake 25 to 30 minutes.

6. Cool 10 minutes before removing from tins.

Per muffin: Calories: 139, Protein: 4 gm., Carbohydrates: 26 gm., Fat: 1 gm., Percentage of calories from fat: 6%

Chapatis

Yields 12 chapatis
PREP TIME: 10 minutes
COOKING TIME: 20 to 25 minutes

Chapatis are a popular, whole wheat flat bread served in India with curries and dal. Similar to a tortilla, this versatile bread is prepared with no oil.

2 cups chapati flour (atta) or whole wheat pastry flour

½ teaspoon salt

1 cup water

extra flour for rolling chapatis

1. Combine flour and salt in a mixing bowl. Slowly pour in up to ⅔ cups water, stirring with one hand to form a soft, kneadable dough. Turn dough onto a clean, flat surface, and knead 5 to 8 minutes. Add more flour or water as needed to form a smooth, pliable dough. Cover with plastic or an overturned bowl, and allow dough to rest 30 minutes.

2. Knead dough again for 1 minute. Divide into 1 dozen balls of equal size, and cover with a damp cloth.

3. Heat a griddle or non-stick frying pan on medium-low. To form chapatis, flatten a ball of dough, dredge in flour, and roll out with a rolling pin into a thin, even disk about 6 inches in diameter.

4. Shake off excess flour, place on a hot griddle, and cook 1 minute on first side. Flip chapati with a spatula, and cook until small, brown spots appear on the underside. Occasionally press chapati down with spatula, and allow air bubbles to rise between layers of dough. Stack cooked chapatis on plate, and cover with towel to keep warm and soft.

Per chapati: Calories: 67, Protein: 3 gm., Carbohydrates: 13 gm., Fat: 0 gm., Percentage of calories from fat: 0%

Corn-Oat Quick Bread

Yields 1 loaf
PREP TIME: 20 minutes
COOKING TIME: 1 hour

This wholesome bread is satisfying with any meal, especially hearty soups and stews.

1 cup soymilk

¼ cup honey

½ cup water

2 tablespoons canola oil

1 tablespoon tamari

¾ cup whole wheat flour

¼ cup unbleached white flour

1 tablespoon baking powder

1 teaspoon salt

1 cup cornmeal

½ cup rolled oats

½ cup onion, minced

2 cloves garlic, minced

1½ teaspoons dried basil

1. Preheat oven to 350°F.

2. In a medium saucepan, heat soymilk, honey, and water until honey is dissolved but liquid does not boil. Stir in oil and tamari.

3. In a mixing bowl, sift together flours, baking powder, and salt. Mix in cornmeal, oats, onion, garlic, and basil. Gradually stir liquid ingredients into the flour mixture. Pour into an oiled loaf or square pan, and bake for 45 minutes to 1 hour.

Per slice (8 per loaf): Calories: 210, Protein: 5 gm., Carbohydrates: 36 gm., Fat: 4 gm., Percentage of calories from fat: 17%

Country Corn Bread

Serves 6
PREP TIME: 20 minutes
COOKING TIME: 35 to 45 minutes

A light, cake-like corn bread that's moist and delicious.

1 cup cornmeal

½ cup whole wheat flour

½ cup wheat germ

2 teaspoons baking powder

1 teaspoon salt

1½ cups soymilk

2 tablespoons honey or rice syrup

1. Preheat oven to 375°F.

2. In a large mixing bowl combine cornmeal, flour, wheat germ, baking powder, and salt.

3 Mix soymilk and honey in a blender or by hand until frothy.

4. Add liquid ingredients to dry mixture, and mix batter.

5. Pour batter into an oiled baking pan, and bake 35 to 45 minutes. Insert knife into the center; when it comes out clean, corn bread is done.

Per serving: Calories: 195, Protein: 7 gm., Carbohydrates: 35 gm., Fat: 2 gm., Percentage of calories from fat: 9%

Cranberry Walnut Bread

Yields 2 half loaves
PREP TIME: 30 minutes
COOKING TIME: 1 hour

This is a great holiday bread. During the seasons when cranberries are not available, you may substitute fresh blueberries or pitted cherries.

2½ cups whole wheat pastry flour

1 teaspoon baking powder

½ teaspoon baking soda

½ teaspoon salt

1 cup soft tofu

1 cup pineapple-orange juice concentrate

½ cup honey

1 teaspoon vanilla extract

1 cup ripe bananas, mashed

1½ cups fresh cranberries

1 tablespoon orange rind, finely grated

1½ cups walnuts, large pieces

1. Preheat oven to 350°F.

2. Combine flour, baking powder, baking soda, and salt in a large bowl.

3. Blend tofu, juice, honey, vanilla, egg replacer, and bananas in food processor.

4. Stir tofu mixture into flour mixture, and blend well with a large wooden spoon. Fold in cranberries, orange rind, and nuts.

5. Divide the batter into two 8-inch, oiled loaf pans, and bake for 1 hour or until a toothpick inserted in the center comes out clean.

6. Cool for 30 minutes before removing from pan.

Per slice (6 per loaf): Calories: 300, Protein: 7 gm., Carbohydrates: 45 gm., Fat: 9 gm., Percentage of calories from fat: 27%

Crispy Southern Corn Bread

Serves 6
PREP TIME: 20 minutes
COOKING TIME: 20 to 30 minutes

This vegan version of corn bread will please any true Southerner. Using a cast-iron skillet gives it an authentic, crispy texture.

¼ cup canola oil

½ pound tofu

1 cup soymilk

egg replacer equivalent to 2 eggs (optional)

¼ cup of honey

3 cups cornmeal

1 cup whole wheat flour

4 teaspoons baking powder

1 teaspoon baking soda

1 teaspoon salt

¼ cup fresh or frozen corn kernels, thawed

¼ cup green chilies, diced, with seeds removed

1. Preheat oven to 375°F.

2. Pour oil in a cast iron skillet or 9" x 12" pan, and place in oven until oil is hot.

3. Mix tofu, soymilk, egg replacer, and honey together in a blender or food processor.

4. In a large mixing bowl, combine cornmeal, flour, baking powder, baking soda, and salt.

5. Add soy mixture, corn kernels, chilies, and heated oil to dry ingredients, and stir.

6. Pour mixture in back into heated skillet, and bake 20 to 30 minutes. Cool before cutting.

Per serving: Calories: 490, Protein: 12 gm., Carbohydrates: 82 gm., Fat: 12 gm., Percentage of calories from fat: 29%

Five Spice Italian Baguette

Yields 2 to 3 loaves
PREP TIME: 1 hour
COOKING TIME: 30 to 40 minutes

This aromatic bread is the perfect companion to simple Italian meals such as lasagne or spaghetti.

2 tablespoons dry active yeast

3 cups warm water

1 tablespoon honey

7½ cups unbleached white flour

1 cup whole wheat flour

2 teaspoons salt

1 tablespoon fresh garlic, minced

2 teaspoons dried basil,
or 1 tablespoon fresh basil, minced

2 teaspoons dried oregano,
or 1 tablespoon fresh oregano, minced

2 teaspoons dried thyme,
or 1 tablespoon fresh thyme, minced

1 teaspoon dried rosemary,
or 2 teaspoons fresh rosemary, minced

1. Whisk together yeast, warm water, honey, and ½ cup flour. Allow to stand 5 minutes until foamy.

2. Add whole wheat flour, remaining white flour, salt, garlic, and herbs to yeast mixture, and blend well. Knead dough 8 minutes, adding more flour if necessary to form a soft, pliable ball.

3. Divide dough into three portions, and shape each into a ball. Let sit undisturbed, covered with a large plastic bag, until doubled in size. Handling dough gently, lightly form into loaves of desired shapes, and place on a flat cookie sheet to bake. For long baguettes, roll dough into loaves using a tight tugging motion.

4. Preheat oven to 400°F.

5. Bake without a second rising on the center rack of the oven 30 to 40 minutes until loaves are golden. Rotate the baking sheet after 15 minutes for even baking.

Per slice (8 per loaf): Calories: 174, Protein: 5 gm., Carbohydrates: 37 gm., Fat: 0 gm., Percentage of calories from fat: 0%

Honey Walnut Quick Bread

Yields 1 loaf
PREP TIME: 15 minutes
COOKING TIME: 1 hour

A rich-tasting quick bread that's made without butter. Serve for breakfast with fruit jam or as an accompaniment to soup and salad.

1 cup soymilk

⅓ cup honey

2 tablespoons canola oil

1½ cups unbleached white flour

1 cup whole wheat flour

1 tablespoon baking powder

1 teaspoon salt

½ cup wheat germ

1 cup walnuts, coarsely chopped

1. Preheat oven to 350°F.

2. In a medium saucepan, heat soymilk and honey until the honey is dissolved, but do not boil. Stir in oil.

3. In a mixing bowl, sift together flours, baking powder, and salt. Add wheat germ. Gradually stir in soymilk and honey mixture. Add walnuts and turn into an oiled loaf pan. Bake for 1 hour.

Per slice (12): Calories: 221, Protein: 6 gm., Carbohydrates: 29 gm., Fat: 9 gm., Percentage of calories from fat: 37%

Honey Whole Wheat Bread

Yields 3 loaves
PREP TIME: 1¾ hours
COOKING TIME: 45 minutes

This is a dense, 100% percent whole wheat bread with the texture of a European loaf. Delicious for toast or hot from the oven with soup and salad.

2 packages dry active yeast

½ cup honey

2½ -3 cups warm water

7½ cups whole wheat flour

1 teaspoon salt

¼ cup canola oil

3 tablespoons sesame seeds

1. Combine yeast, honey, and 2½ cups warm water in a small bowl, and mix well. Leave the bowl undisturbed in a warm place for 10 minutes until the yeast mixture is frothy.

2. Combine flour and salt in large bowl. Add yeast mixture and canola oil. Mix with a wooden spoon until well-combined. Add additional ½ cup warm water if dough feels stiff and dry.

3. Turn dough onto a floured board, and knead for 8 to 10 minutes until dough is smooth and elastic.

4. Wash and oil the mixing bowl. Roll dough into a ball, coat lightly with oil, and place back in the bowl. Cover and allow dough to rise in a warm place for 1 hour until doubled in size.

5. Preheat oven to 375°F.

6. Punch down dough with your fist, and knead lightly. Shape into three loaves. Place the loaves in oiled loaf pans, and cover. Leave dough undisturbed in a warm place for 30 minutes or until doubled again.

7. Sprinkle with sesame seeds and bake in a hot oven for 45 minutes. Bread is done when it turns golden and makes a hollow sound when tapped. Remove loaves from oven, and cool for at least 10 minutes before removing from pans.

Per slice (8 per loaf): Calories: 173, Protein: 5 gm., Carbohydrates: 30 gm., Fat: 3 gm., Percentage of calories from fat: 16%

Oat n' Honey Tahini Wheat Bread

Yields 3 loaves
PREP TIME: 1 hour
COOKING TIME: 1 hour

2 cups hot water

2 cups rolled oats

4 tablespoons honey

4 tablespoons tahini

4 tablespoons dry powdered yeast

1 cup warm water

4 cups whole wheat flour

4 cups unbleached white flour

2 teaspoons salt

1. Combine hot water and rolled oats, and let stand 5 minutes. Add honey and tahini, and whisk together.

2. Dissolve yeast in warm water, and add to oat mixture.

3. Add oat mixture and salt to flours. Mix well and knead 8 minutes. If dough is sticky, add a few handfuls of dry oats.

4. Place dough in a clean bowl, cover with plastic or a towel, and set in a warm place until doubled in size (approximately 30 minutes). Punch down, then shape into 3 to 4 loaves.

5. Place loaves, seam side down, in lightly oiled bread pans. Brush tops of loaves with a mixture of 4 tablespoons water and 4 tablespoons honey, and sprinkle with dry oats. Allow to rise a second time (approximately 30 minutes).

6. Preheat oven to 400°F.

7. Bake on the center rack for 45 to 60 minutes until crust is browned and bread sounds hollow when tapped.

Per slice (8 per loaf): Calories: 192, Protein: 7 gm., Carbohydrates: 36 gm., Fat: 2 gm., Percentage of calories from fat: 9%

Potato Onion Bread

Yields 3 loaves
PREP TIME: 1¾ to 2 hours
COOKING TIME: 40 to 50 minutes

This distinctive bread makes wonderful toast, garlic bread, or sandwich slices.

2 packages dry yeast

2 cups warm water

3 tablespoons honey

1 tablespoon salt

3 tablespoons oil

2 medium potatoes, boiled and mashed well

¾ cup onion, finely chopped

6-7 cups unbleached white flour

1. In a large mixing bowl, dissolve yeast in warm water. Add honey, salt, oil, mashed potatoes, and onions, and mix well. Gradually add 3 cups of flour, and stir vigorously.

2. Add remaining flour a little at a time until dough becomes stiff.

3. Turn dough onto floured board, and knead 10 to 15 minutes until smooth and elastic. Add more flour if needed.

4. Wash and oil the mixing bowl. Roll dough into a ball, coat lightly with oil, and place back in the bowl. Cover and allow dough to rise in a warm spot for 1 hour until doubled in size.

5. Punch down dough and knead lightly. Cover and allow to rise once again until doubled in size.

6. Punch dough down again and turn onto a lightly floured board. Divide into thirds and shape into three loaves. Place in oiled loaf pans, and cover. Place loaves in a warm spot, and let rise another 30 minutes or until doubled in size.

7. Preheat oven to 350°F.

8. Bake for 40 to 50 minutes. Bread is done when crust turns golden and loaf makes a hollow sound when tapped. Remove loaves from the oven, and cool at least 10 minutes before removing from pans.

Per slice (24): Calories: 153, Protein: 4 gm., Carbohydrates: 30 gm., Fat: 2 gm., Percentage of calories from fat: 12%

Savory Vegetable-Filled Bread

Yields 3 loaves
PREP TIME: 2 hours
COOKING TIME: 1 hour

FILLING:

1 medium onion, minced

6 cloves garlic, minced

1 medium eggplant or zucchini, minced

1 green pepper, minced

6 sun-dried tomatoes, soaked 30 minutes, drained, and minced

2 tablespoons tamari

½ cup water

1 tablespoon basil

1 teaspoon salt

pinch black pepper

DOUGH:

2 packages dry active yeast

½ cup honey

2 cups warm water

7½ cups whole wheat flour

1 teaspoon salt

¼ cup canola oil

Per slice (8 per loaf): Calories: 184, Protein: 5 gm., Carbohydrates: 33 gm., Fat: 2 gm., Percentage of calories from fat: 10%

1. Combine all filling ingredients in a saucepan. Cook, covered, over medium heat 10 minutes. Uncover and cook 5 minutes or more to reduce liquid. Drain excess juices. Set aside.

2. To make dough, combine yeast, honey, and warm water in a small bowl and mix well. Leave the bowl undisturbed in a warm place 5 minutes until yeast mixture is frothy.

3. Combine flour and salt in a large bowl. Add yeast and oil, and mix with a wooden spoon until well-combined.

4. Turn dough onto a floured board, and knead 8 to 10 minutes until dough is smooth and elastic.

5. Wash and oil the mixing bowl. Roll dough into a ball, coat lightly with oil, and place back in the bowl. Cover and allow dough to rise in a warm spot for 1 hour until doubled in size.

6. Preheat oven to 375°F.

7. Punch down dough and knead again lightly. Divide dough evenly into 3 balls. With a rolling pin, roll one ball into a large square. Spread ⅓ of the filling over the dough. Roll dough around filling and pinch ends closed. Repeat with remaining balls of dough. Place loaves in oiled pans, and cover. Set in a warm spot, and let rise 30 minutes or until dough doubles in size.

8. Bake for 45 minutes. Bread is done when crust turns golden and loaf sounds hollow when tapped. Remove loaves from oven and turn bread out onto a cooling rack.

Sour Dough Rye Bread

Yields 2 loaves
PREP TIME: 20 minutes
COOKING TIME: 1 hour and 15 minutes

This light, flavorful bread is simple to make. Serve with hearty soups such as Ashram Lentil Soup (page 42) or Winter's Eve Potato Chowder (page 58).

2 tablespoons dry active yeast

2½ cups warm water

1½ cups sour dough starter (room temperature)

5½ cups unbleached white flour

3 cups rye flour

1 tablespoon salt

2 tablespoons honey

4 tablespoons caraway or anise seeds

1. Combine yeast with warm water and sour dough starter. Stir and allow to stand 5 minutes until foamy. Add remaining ingredients, using enough white flour to make a soft ball. Knead 8 to 10 minutes.

2. Place dough in a large bowl. Cover with a damp towel, and set in warm place 30 minutes or until doubled in size. Punch down and roll into a ball. Let dough relax 5 minutes.

3. Preheat oven to 400°F.

4. Punch down again and form into 2 to 3 loaves. Place loaves seam side down in lightly oiled pans.

5. Bake on the center oven rack for 45 minutes until crust is browned and bread sounds hollow when tapped.

Per slice (8 per loaf): Calories: 152, Protein: 6 gm., Carbohydrates: 30 gm., Fat: 0 gm., Percentage of calories from fat: 0%

Sour Dough Starter

Yields enough for 2 to 3 loaves
PREP TIME: 5 minutes

Use this simple starter for making sour dough breads.

1 cup warm water

1 cup unbleached white flour

⅛ teaspoon dry active yeast

Mix together water, flour, and yeast. Allow to sit at room temperature, loosely covered, for 24 hours. After fermentation, cover well and refrigerate. Use within 7 days.

Toasted Seed And Nut Bread

Yields 2 Loaves
PREP TIME: 20 minutes
COOKING TIME: 1 hour and 15 minutes

This hearty bread is packed with nutrients and lots of flavor.

2 tablespoons dry active yeast

3 cups warm water

3 tablespoons honey

3 tablespoons tamari

4 tablespoons whole cumin seeds

3 tablespoons sesame seeds

1 tablespoon black mustard seeds

1 cup roasted pumpkin seeds

1 cup roasted peanuts, finely chopped

5 cups whole wheat flour

3-4 cups unbleached white flour

1. Toast cumin, sesame, and mustard seeds in a skillet over a medium-high flame. Stir until seeds "pop" and turn golden.

2. Combine yeast with warm water and 1 cup white flour. Stir and allow to stand 5 minutes until foamy. Add 5 cups whole wheat flour and mix. Add all other ingredients, adding enough white flour to make a soft ball. Knead 8 to 10 minutes.

3. Place dough in a large bowl. Cover with a damp towel, and set in a warm place 30 minutes or until dough doubles in size. Punch down and roll into a ball. Let dough relax 5 minutes. Punch down again and form into 2 loaves. Place loaves seam side down in lightly oiled pans.

4. Bake on the center rack of a 400°F oven 45 minutes until crust is brown and bread sounds hollow when tapped.

Per slice (12 per loaf): Calories: 227, Protein: 8 gm., Carbohydrates: 36 gm., Fat: 6 gm., Percentage of calories from fat: 24%

Whole Wheat Molasses Corn Loaf

Yields 2 loaves
PREP TIME: 1 hour
COOKING TIME: 1 hour

This sweet, dense bread is simple to prepare and makes a hearty meal when served with soups and salads.

2 tablespoons dry powdered yeast

3 cups warm water (105°F to 110°F)

3 tablespoons molasses

4 cups whole wheat flour, with extra for kneading

1 cup unbleached white flour

1½ cups yellow cornmeal

1 teaspoon salt

2 tablespoons honey

2 tablespoons water

1. Combine yeast, water, and molasses in a large stainless steel bowl. Add ½ cup flour. Whisk and let stand 5 minutes. Add remaining whole wheat and unbleached flours, cornmeal, and salt. Mix, then knead for 5 minutes on a floured surface.

2. Form dough into a ball, place in a clean, lightly oiled bowl, and cover with towel. Allow to rise in a warm place for 15 minutes (not until doubled). Punch down risen dough and shape into 2 loaves. Place seam side down in lightly oiled bread pans.

3. Allow dough to rise again uncovered in a warm place for 20 to 30 minutes until almost doubled in size. For a crispy, sweet crust, brush loaves with a mixture of 2 tablespoons honey and 2 tablespoons warm water before baking.

4. Bake at 400°F for 40 minutes or until top is golden brown and bread sounds hollow when tapped.

Per slice (12 per loaf): Calories: 131, Protein: 4 gm., Carbohydrates: 28 gm., Fat: 0 gm., Percentage of calories from fat: 0%

DESSERTS

It is said that the Kundalini Shakti loves sugar, and somehow this irresistible sweet tooth manifests after a strong meditation class. We don't suggest you eat a lot of sugar, but you needn't feel guilty about an occasional indulgence in birthday cake and ice cream. These recipes include fruit-sweetened desserts, some light and others rich-tasting. We do break the rules almost every Sunday brunch with our luscious Ganeshapuri Fruit Salad.

Almond Figs

Serves 6
PREP TIME: 30 minutes

If fresh figs are not available, use dried figs that have been simmered in brandy or apple juice until tender.

12 fresh figs, peeled

12 whole blanched almonds

½ cup almond or fruit brandy or apple juice

1½ cups soy yogurt

2 teaspoons honey

1. Press whole almonds into each fig. Lay figs side by side in a shallow dish, and marinate in brandy or apple juice for at least 1 hour.

2. Combine yogurt and honey with brandy or juice from marinade. Pour yogurt into 6 chilled champagne or dessert glasses, and top each with 2 stuffed figs. Served chilled.

Per serving: Calories: 155, Protein: 2 gm., Carbohydrates: 21 gm., Fat: 2 gm., Percentage of calories from fat: 12%

Baklava

Yields 2 dozen 2½" squares
PREP TIME: 45 minutes
COOKING TIME: 40-50 minutes

This "break the rules" dessert is irresistibly sweet with a wholesome nut 'n honey flavor.

½ pound soy margarine

1 pound walnuts

½ pound pecans

1½ cups honey

¼ cup orange liqueur,
 or the juice of 1 fresh orange and 1
 tablespoon grated orange rind

1 teaspoon cinnamon

¼ teaspoon cardamom

1 (1 pound) box filo pastry

1. Melt margarine in a small saucepan. Allow to sit in a warm place for 30 minutes until the clarified oil separates from the white solids.

2. Finely grind half the nuts in a food processor, or finely chop by hand. Combine with the remaining nuts.

3. Make a syrup by combining honey, orange liqueur or juice and rind, cinnamon, and cardamom in a saucepan, and heat. Set aside in a warm place.

4. Lay the filo sheets out flat and cover with plastic wrap to prevent drying. Using a soft pastry brush and only the clarified portion of melted margarine, lightly brush the surface of a 10" x 15" cookie sheet or glass baking pan. Lay the first sheet of filo down flat into the pan. Brush top lightly with clarified margarine, and lay second sheet of filo over the first, again brushing lightly with margarine. Repeat for third layer. Sprinkle ⅔ of the nut mixture over these three layers of filo. Repeat process two more times using the remaining nuts on top of final layer. Then use the remaining filo to cover the third layer of nuts. There will be many more layers to continue layering one at a time with light brushes of margarine.

5. Preheat oven to 350°F.

6. Cut the unbaked pan of Baklava into diamond shapes or squares (it crumbles and breaks if cut after baking), and bake for 40 to 50 minutes. Cool and top with hot syrup before serving.

Per serving: Calories: 594, Protein: 7 gm., Carbohydrates: 55 gm., Fat: 37 gm., Percentage of calories from fat: 56%

Banana Oatmeal Cookies

Yields 2½ dozen 2¾" cookies
PREP TIME: 20 minutes
COOKING TIME: 15 minutes

A wholesome treat that's not overly sweet.

2 cups banana, mashed

¼ cup apple juice concentrate

½ cup honey

egg replacer equivalent to 2 eggs (optional)

2 tablespoons oil

½ teaspoon salt

3 cups rolled oats

1 cup whole wheat pastry flour

2 teaspoons baking soda

1 cup raisins

1. In a large mixing bowl combine bananas, juice, honey, egg replacer, and oil.

2. In a separate bowl, combine salt, oats, flour, baking soda, and raisins.

3. Add dry ingredients to wet mixture, and stir well.

4. Preheat oven to 350°F.

5. Drop by spoonfuls onto a lightly oiled cookie sheet, and bake 12 to 15 minutes or until golden brown.

Per cookie: Calories: 97, Protein: 2 gm., Carbohydrates: 19 gm., Fat: 2 gm., Percentage of calories from fat: 19%

Bhirnee

Serves 6 to 8
PREP TIME: 20 minutes
COOKING TIME: 20 minutes

This creamy rice and almond pudding is an Indian sweet made with fragrant basmati rice and rosewater, found in Middle Eastern and Asian markets.

¾ cup uncooked basmati rice

¼ cup honey

1½ quarts plain or vanilla soymilk

1 teaspoon rosewater

¼ cup slivered almonds, toasted

1. Rinse rice in cold water. Drain and soak in enough cold water to barely cover for 2 hours. In a blender or food processor, grind the rice until coarsely chopped.

2. In a large saucepan, bring milk and honey to a boil. Mix ground rice with boiled milk, and bring to a boil again. Reduce heat and simmer 15 minutes. Remove from heat, stir in rosewater, and spoon rice mixture into individual serving dishes or custard cups.

3. Garnish each serving with toasted almonds and chill for at least one hour. Pudding will thicken slightly.

Per serving: Calories: 186, Protein: 7 gm., Carbohydrates: 25 gm., Fat: 7 gm., Percentage of calories from fat: 34%

Cardamom Spice Cake

Serves 10 to 12
PREP TIME: 20 minutes
COOKING TIME: 40 minutes

Cardamom is a sweet spice that lends a pleasing flavor to baking.

½ cup raisins

3 cups whole wheat pastry flour

½ teaspoon salt

3 teaspoons baking soda

1 teaspoon vanilla

1 teaspoon cardamom

½ teaspoon cinnamon

¼ teaspoon cloves

¼ teaspoon nutmeg

1 cup honey

¾ cup apple juice concentrate

¼ cup orange juice concentrate

⅔ cup water

1. In a large mixing bowl, combine raisins, flour, salt, and baking soda.

2. Whisk together vanilla, cardamom, cinnamon, cloves, nutmeg, honey, juices, and water.

3. Pour liquid ingredients into dry mixture and blend well.

4. Preheat oven to 350°F.

5. Spread batter into an oiled 9" x 13" pan. Bake for 40 minutes or until cake pulls away from sides of pan.

Per serving: Calories: 243, Protein: 4 gm., Carbohydrates: 56 gm., Fat: 0 gm., Percentage of calories from fat: 0%

Carrot Date Bars

Yields 1 dozen 3" x 3¼" bars
PREP TIME: 25 minutes
COOKING TIME: 45 minutes

These chewy, fruit-sweetened bars are a healthy energy boost.

egg replacer equivalent to 4 eggs (optional)

½ cup orange juice concentrate

½ cup apple juice concentrate

½ cup honey

2 teaspoons cinnamon

2 cups carrots, grated

**2½ cups unbleached white flour or whole
    wheat pastry flour,
    or 1¼ cups of each**

2 teaspoons baking soda

½ cup walnuts, coarsely chopped

½ cup dates, chopped

¾ cup shredded coconut

1. In a large mixing bowl, whisk together egg replacer, fruit juices, honey, cinnamon, and carrots.

2. In a separate bowl, combine dry ingredients except coconut.

3. Pour liquid ingredients into dry mixture, and blend well.

4. Preheat oven to 350°F.

5. Spread batter into an oiled 9" x 13" pan, and sprinkle with coconut. Bake for 45 minutes or until bars are completely cooked in the center.

Per bar: Calories: 319, Protein: 5 gm., Carbohydrates: 49 gm., Fat: 11 gm., Percentage of calories from fat: 31%

Chai

Yields 6 cups
PREP TIME: 10 minutes
COOKING TIME: 10 minutes

Everyone loves this Indian spiced tea. Our healthful version is pleasing after meals or for tea time and is delicious served cold in the summer.

3 cups water

3 cups soymilk

8-10 bags black tea (preferably Darjeeling) or decaffeinated black tea

½ cup honey

1 teaspoon ground cinnamon

1 teaspoon ground cardamom

½ teaspoon ground nutmeg

½ teaspoon ground clove

½ teaspoon ground ginger

pinch black pepper

In a large pot, bring water and soymilk to a boil. Add tea bags, honey, and spices. Bring to a boil, turn off flame, then steep for 3 to 5 minutes. Remove tea bags, pour through fine mesh strainer, and serve.

Per cup: Calories: 111, Protein: 2 gm., Carbohydrates: 21 gm., Fat: 1 gm., Percentage of calories from fat: 8%

Fresh Strawberry Tofu Pie

Yields one 9" pie (8 slices)
PREP TIME: 30 minutes
COOKING TIME: 1 hour

This luscious dessert is just like fresh strawberries and cream, but without the calories.

2 cups granola

3 tablespoons apple juice

1 pound soft tofu

2 tablespoons fresh lemon juice

1½ teaspoons pure vanilla extract

pinch salt

2 cups fresh strawberries, chopped

½ cup honey

2 cups fresh strawberries, sliced

⅔ cup honey

1 tablespoon arrowroot powder

1. Preheat oven to 350°F.

2. Combine granola and apple juice in a blender, and process until the mixture has a fine, crumb-like texture. Pat into a 9" glass pie plate, and bake for 10 minutes or until golden brown. Allow to cool. Preheat oven to same temperature before starting filling.

3. Puree tofu, lemon juice, vanilla, salt, chopped strawberries, and ½ cup honey until smooth.

4. Pour filling into pie crust, and bake for 1 hour or until edges turn golden.

5. In a small saucepan, combine sliced strawberries with ⅔ cup honey, and add water just to cover. Bring to a boil and thicken with arrowroot powder. Serve warm sauce over freshly baked pie.

Per slice: Calories: 317, Protein: 7 gm., Carbohydrates: 50 gm., Fat: 10 gm., Percentage of calories from fat: 28%

Ganeshapuri Fruit Salad

Serves 6 to 8
PREP TIME: 30 minutes

This salad is named after the town where Bhagawan Nityananda lived. It's so much like ambrosia or the nectar of gods that it's usually served at Bhandaras (Indian feasts) or other special occasions. We serve it almost every Sunday at Shoshoni with enthusiastic approval from everyone. You may substitute any of these suggested fruits with others that are ripe and in season.

1 peach, chopped

1 red or green apple, chopped

¾ cup strawberries, halved

½ cup bananas, sliced

½ cup seedless red or green grapes

½ cup fresh blueberries

½ cup fresh raspberries, blackberries, or boysenberries

¼ cup honey

1½ cups soy yogurt

½ teaspoon cardamom

½ cup coconut, toasted

½ cup slivered almonds, toasted

¾ cup assorted chocolates (chocolate chips, kisses, M &Ms, or whatever you fancy)

1. In a large mixing bowl, combine peaches, apples, ½ cup strawberries, bananas, grapes, blueberries, and other berries.

2. Puree ¼ cup strawberries, honey, soy yogurt, and cardamom.

3. Stir yogurt dressing into fruit, and mix well. Stir in coconut, almonds, and chocolates. Chill and let sit 1 hour before serving.

Per serving: Calories: 387, Protein: 5 gm., Carbohydrates: 42 gm., Fat: 21 gm., Percentage of calories from fat: 49%

Mandarin Orange Sauce

Yields 2 cups
PREP TIME: 10 minutes
COOKING TIME: 10 minutes

A delicious topping for Cardamom Spice Cake (page 193) or Orange-Almond Gateau (page 199).

1 cup orange juice

½ cup apple juice

3 tablespoons cornstarch

1 teaspoon almond extract

1 cup fresh or canned mandarin orange slices

¼ cup slivered almonds, toasted

1. In a small saucepan combine juices. Whisk in cornstarch. Slowly heat and stir until sauce thickens to a pudding-like consistency. Whisk in almond extract.

2. Remove from heat and allow to cool before topping cake. Garnish with mandarin orange slices and almonds.

Per ¼ cup: Calories: 79, Protein: 1 gm., Carbohydrates: 13 gm., Fat: 3 gm., Percentage of calories from fat: 34%

Orange-Almond Gateau

Serves 4
PREP TIME: 30 minutes
COOKING TIME: 30 minutes

This light cake is delightful sliced into lady fingers and served with a dollop of Raspberry Mousse (page 201) or iced with Mandarin Orange Sauce (page 198).

egg replacer equivalent to 4 large eggs

½ cup applesauce

1 tablespoon water

¾ cup orange juice concentrate

⅔ cup orange juice

1 cup whole wheat flour

1 cup unbleached white flour

1 teaspoon almond extract

1 teaspoon baking soda

2½ teaspoons baking powder

1. Preheat oven to 350°F.

2. Combine egg replacer, applesauce, water, and juices. Beat with a whisk. Add almond extract and stir.

3. Add flours to liquid ingredients, and mix well. Add baking soda and baking powder, and mix in gently. Pour into a 13" x 9" x 2" pan, and bake for 30 minutes. Allow to cool before cutting.

Per serving: Calories: 271, Protein: 9 gm., Carbohydrates: 57 gm., Fat: 0 gm., Percentage of calories from fat: 0%

Pineapple Carob Cashew Brownies

Yields 1 dozen 3" x 3¼" brownies
PREP TIME: 20 minutes
COOKING TIME: 1 hour

These fruit-sweetened brownies satisfy a chocolate craving with their rich taste and moist, chewy texture.

2 cups whole wheat pastry flour,
   or 1 cup unbleached white flour and 1
   cup whole wheat flour

⅔ cup carob powder

2 teaspoons baking powder

pinch salt

½ cup honey or apple juice concentrate

½ cup unsweetened applesauce

¼ cup pineapple juice concentrate

1 cup canned unsweetened pineapple pieces
   with their natural juice

1 teaspoon vanilla

½ cup raw cashew pieces

1. Preheat oven to 350°F.

2. In a large mixing bowl combine flour, carob, baking powder, and salt.

3. Blend honey, applesauce, juices, pineapple, and vanilla.

4. Add dry ingredients to wet mixture, and stir in nuts. Pour batter into an oiled 9" x 13" pan. Bake for 1 hour or until brownies pull away from sides of pan.

Per brownie: Calories: 172, Protein: 4 gm., Carbohydrates: 31 gm., Fat: 4 gm., Percentage of calories from fat: 20%

Raspberry Mousse

Serves 6 to 8
PREP TIME: 10 minutes

A light and refreshing fruit-sweetened dessert that tastes like sherbert. Serve alone or with Orange-Almond Gateau lady fingers.

3 tablespoons agar flakes

¼ cup raspberry juice

3 cups fresh raspberries or unsweetened frozen raspberries, thawed and drained

1 (10½ ounce) package silken tofu

3 tablespoons raspberry jam or honey

2 tablespoons fresh orange juice

1. Heat raspberry juice in a small saucepan, and whisk in agar flakes. Bring to a boil and then simmer for 3 to 4 minutes until agar is completely dissolved. Cool to room temperature.

2. Puree all ingredients in a food processor or blender until silky smooth.

3. Spoon mousse into a serving bowl or parfait glasses, and chill 1 to 2 hours until set. Serve with tofu whipped cream and fresh raspberries.

Per serving: Calories: 92, Protein: 3 gm., Carbohydrates: 15 gm., Fat: 1 gm., Percentage of calories from fat: 10%

Walnut Raisin Cookies

Yields 3 dozen 2" cookies
PREP TIME: 20 minutes
COOKING TIME: 15 minutes

These cookies are reminiscent of old-fashioned ice box cookies.

3 cups unbleached white flour

2 teaspoons baking powder

¼ teaspoon salt

½ cup honey or maple syrup

⅔ cup canola oil

2 teaspoons natural vanilla extract

½ cup walnuts, finely chopped

¼ cup raisins

1. Sift together flour, baking powder, and salt.

2. In a separate bowl, whisk together honey, oil, and vanilla extract until light and foamy. Combine with flour mixture and mix well. Fold in walnuts and raisins.

3. Roll dough into ropes about 1-inch thick, and cover with plastic. Refrigerate at least 3 hours or overnight.

4. Preheat oven to 350°F.

5. Slice chilled dough in ½-inch circles, roll into balls, and arrange on a baking sheet. Bake 10 minutes or until cookies turn golden.

Per cookie: Calories: 81, Protein: 1 gm., Carbohydrates: 13 gm., Fat: 2 gm., Percentage of calories from fat: 22%

GOING ALL OUT MENUS

Holiday Menu

Royal Tofu Roulade
Wild Rice Stuffing
Christmas Cranberry Glaze
Miniature Harvest Pumpkins
filled with Creamed Swiss Chard
fresh steamed asparagus
Orange-Almond Gateau

Special Occasion

Avocado Mint Salad
Shiitake Consomme with
Greens
Polenta Torta
Raspberry Mousse

Far Eastern Feast

San Francisco Pot Stickers
Ginger-Tamari Sauce
Hot N' Sour Miso Soup
Mandarin Tofu
brown rice
Cardamom Spice Cake

Fiesta Feast

Blue Corn Empanadas
Zucchini-Pine Nut Tamales
Pico de Gallo
Guacamole
Pinto Beans
Ole! Pozole
Pineapple Carob Cashew Brownies

Indian Feast

Samosas
Date Chutney
Festival Rice
Sweet Corn and Coconut Curry
Lentil Sambar
Chapatis
Bhirnee
Chai

Near Eastern Feast

Dolmades
Hummus with pita slices
Imam Bayeldi
Mudjedera
Baklava

SEASONAL FARE MENUS

Spring

Asparagus Spring Rolls
Tamari-Orange Dressing
Marinated Artichokes
Early Spring Primavera

Summer

Black Bean and Fresh Corn Summer Salad
Avocado Gazpacho
Kolokethopita
Fresh Strawberry Tofu Pie

Autumn

Apple-Beet Borscht
Brussels Sprouts Salad
Stuffed Swiss Chard with Carrot Sauce
Honey Whole Wheat Bread
Butternut Squash Spread

Winter

Root Stew
Sesame Soba Noodles
Oriental Slaw

Menus

	Breakfast	Lunch	Dinner
Day 1	Aloha Muffins, *pg. 171* Fruit ' Nut Granola, *pg. 24* soymilk	Spanakopita, *pg. 137* Tabouli, *pg. 73* Savory Lentils, *pg. 153*	Black Bean-Avocado Enchila-das, *pg. 112* Ole! Pozole, *pg. 161* Guacamole, *pg. 87*
Day 2	Banana French Toast, *pg. 20* Fresh Strawberry Syrup, *pg. 29*	Carrot Mint Soup, *pg. 44* Supergrain Salad, *pg. 72* Savory Vegetable-Filled Bread, *pg. 183*	Eggplant Rollatini, *pg. 115* Broccoli Pepper Salad, *pg. 63* Five Spice Italian Baguette, *pg. 178*
Day 3	Golden-Baked Breakfast Potatoes, *pg. 25* Honey Walnut Quick Bread, *pg. 179*	Mexican Corn Soup, *pg. 54* Vegetable-Tortilla Fold-Ups, *pg. 141* Anasazi Beans, *pg. 148*	Empress Tofu, *pg. 116* Spicy Peanut Noodles, *pg. 71* brown rice
Day 4	Indian Cereal, *pg. 26* Toasted Seed & Nut Bread, *pg. 186* fruit salad	Tibetan Barley Soup, *pg. 56* Marinated Vegetable Salad, *pg. 67* Carrot Date Bars, *pg. 194*	Mushroom Stroganoff, *pg. 128* Kasha with Raisins and Walnuts, *pg. 160* green salad with Tamari-Orange Dressing, *pg. 104*
Day 5	Brown Rice Pudding, *pg. 23* Blueberry Oatmeal Muffins, *pg. 172*	Pasta Fagioli, *pg. 129* Warm Spinach Salad, *pg. 75* Potato Onion Bread, *pg. 182*	Cauliflower Sabji, *pg. 113* Golden Saffron Rice, *pg. 159* Shoshoni Red Lentil Dal, *pg. 154*
Day 6	Multi-Grain Flapjacks, *pg. 27* Orange-Honey Syrup, *pg. 29* fresh fruit	Fabulous Low-Fat Falafel, *pg. 117* Tahini Sauce, *pg. 83* Eggplant Tomato Relish, *pg. 92*	Garden-Style Stuffed Potatoes, *pg. 118* Ashram Lentil Soup, *pg. 42* green salad with Raspberry Poppy Seed Dressing, *pg. 101*
Day 7	Breakfast Burritos, *pg. 22* Pico De Gallo, *pg. 93*	Creamy White Bean Soup, *pg. 50* Fragrant Rice Salad, *pg. 66* Banana Oatmeal Cookies, *pg. 191*	Layered Vegetable Bake, *pg. 122* Beet Salad with Toasted Walnuts, *pg. 61*
Day 8	Scrambled Tofu, *pg. 28* Honey Whole Wheat Bread, toasted, *pg. 180*	Tofu in a Pocket, *pg. 145* Winter's Eve Potato Chow-der, *pg. 58* Pineapple Carob Cashew Brownies, *pg. 200*	Tempeh Tandoori, *pg. 140* Festival Rice, *pg. 158* Green Beans with Cashews, *pg. 166*

Index

Ask your store to carry these fine Vegan Cookbooks from
the Book Publishing Company

20 Minutes to Dinner $12.95
Almost-No Fat Cookbook 12.95
Almost-No Fat Holiday Cookbook 12.95
Ecological Cooking: Recipes to Save the Planet 10.95
Fabulous Beans 9.95
Fat-Free & Easy 10.00
Good Time Eatin' in Cajun Country 9.95
Health-Promoting Cookbook 12.95
Instead of Chicken, Instead of Turkey 9.95
Judy Brown's Guide to Natural Foods Cooking 10.95
Lighten Up! with Louise Hagler 11.95
Natural Lunchbox 12.95
Nutritional Yeast Cookbook 9.95
Peaceful Palate 15.00
Shoshoni Cookbook 14.95
Solar Cooking 8.95
Soyfoods Cookery 9.95
Sprout Garden 8.95
Table for Two 12.95
Taste of Mexico 13.95
Uncheese Cookbook 11.95
Vegan Vittles 11.95

Vegan Diet & Health Books:

Physician's Slimming Guide . . . . $ 5.95
Power of Your Plate 12.95
Foods That Cause You to Lose Weight *revised edition* . . 12.95

or you may order directly from:

Book Publishing Company
P.O. Box 99
Summertown, TN 38483

Or call: 1-800-695-2241
Please add $2.50 per book for shipping